THE SURVIVOR PERSONALITY

Also available by Patsy Westcott
How to Get What You Want

THE SURVIVOR PERSONALITY

How to get through the bad times and come up smiling

—

Patsy Westcott

BLOOMSBURY

To Jenny Glew

Many people have helped me write this book, both directly and indirectly. In particular, I should like to thank Nicola Gibson, Anna Clements and my daughter, Kate Westcott, who helped me with research. I should also like to thank Rowena Gaunt and Isabelle Auden at Bloomsbury, for suggesting the book to me and bearing with me when I missed my deadline. I'd like to make a special mention of my friend, Jenny Glew, who sadly died while I was writing the final chapters. Jenny was one of life's great survivors. Despite more than her fair share of bad luck – she had both multiple sclerosis and breast cancer – she was unfailingly cheerful, bright and curious – key survivor qualities. While I was writing this book I visited her in hospital and we had a long conversation about *The Survivor Personality*. She invited me to use her experiences in any way I wanted. I would like to believe that Jenny's confidence, her spirit of positive thinking and her way of finding the 'gift' in any situation shine through these pages.

The author and the publisher cannot be held liable for any errors and omissions, or actions that may be taken as a consequence of using it.

All rights reserved: no part of this publication may be reproduced, stored in a retrieval system, or transmitted in any form or by any means, electronic, mechanical, photocopying or otherwise, without the prior written permission of the publisher.

First published 1995 by Bloomsbury publishing Plc, 2 Soho Square, London W1V 6HB

Copyright © 1995 Patsy Westcott

The moral right of the author has been asserted

A copy of the CIP entry for this book is available from the British Library

ISBN 0 7475 2157 3

10 9 8 7 6 5 4 3 2 1

Designed by Hugh Adams, AB3
Typeset by Hewer Text Composition Services, Edinburgh
Printed in Britain by Cox & Wyman Ltd, Reading

CONTENTS

On a personal note   1
Introduction   3

PART ONE Personal power
Chapter one   9
   What makes a survivor?
Chapter two   28
   Body power
Chapter three   41
   Feeling power
Chapter four   59
   People power
Chapter five   76
   Mind power
Chapter six   91
   Good times, bad times

PART TWO Making it work
Chapter seven   107
   Surviving a break up
Chapter eight   125
   Surviving job loss
Chapter nine   137
   Surviving sickness
Chapter ten   155
   Surviving disaster
Chapter eleven   168
   Surviving your future

PART THREE: Inspirations and Information

Chapter twelve   189
    Inspiring people and books

Appendix 1   204
    Who can help?

Appendix 2   210
    Useful addresses

Index   216

ON A PERSONAL NOTE

All of us face difficult times as we go through life. Like many people I didn't find my childhood especially easy or happy. My mother had schizophrenia and was dogged by poor physical health. From the time of her first mental 'breakdown' when I was eight years old to her death from breast cancer when I was 20, she also suffered recurring bouts of depression. During her illnesses I was the person she turned to for support. At times, I felt almost overwhelmed by her needs. Somehow, however, I managed to survive. For me, this book has been a very personal journey as I have discovered the inner strengths which I drew upon at that time and which, I believe, enabled me to survive.

While reading the many papers that have been written on survival and talking to other survivors I realised that I had managed to develop many of the attributes identified by psychologists as 'resilience'. I had strong, nurturing relationships with my grandfather, father, my sister, whom I deeply love and admire, and good friends who made me feel loved and helped me believe in myself. My mother too, in periods when she was well, did her best and, despite her illness, we had a close relationship. I learned much from her about what it means to be vulnerable, and I believe this has given me the ability to empathise with other people who are going through difficult times. Work – and, when I was a child, school – was also a huge resource, enabling me to develop a sense of perspective on what was happening in my life, allowing me periods of escape and giving me the success I needed to maintain confidence in myself.

None of the subsequent challenges I have faced in my life have been quite as confusing as my mother's illness, though like many people I have had my fair share of tough times – a divorce, the break up of important relationships, and the deaths of people I loved.

I believe, however, that during these hard times the things I learnt during my childhood and my belief in my own ability to survive helped me to pull through.

My own experiences, then, gave me the impetus to write *The Survivor Personality*. What I have tried to do throughout the book is to translate and bring to life the insights of psychologists and the things I have found out myself in my life and work, through reflecting on my own experiences and talking to other survivors. I am grateful to the many people – my friends (they know who they are), my sister, my daughters and the teachers, writers and other guides – who I have turned to in times of trouble who have helped me to survive. From these people I have learned all I know about courage, wisdom, strength in the face of adversity and self-reliance. I hope that the insights I have gained, and now offer you, help you in some small way to find your own strength to survive.

INTRODUCTION

I WILL SURVIVE

How would *you* cope if you lost your job, contracted a serious illness or faced a difficult personal crisis? Everyone reacts differently to the slings and arrows life hurls our way. Some sink into despair. Others complain of the unfairness of it all – as if they believed a malicious fate had singled them out as part of some personal vendetta. Others get angry and lash out at those around them. A few, however, reach inside themselves and find ways of turning trouble on its head. These are life's survivors, people with an amazing talent for surmounting change and difficulty and turning bad luck into good luck.

In the public arena, they include those who have survived horrendous experiences such as concentration camps or being taken hostage, to celebrities whose brush with death and destruction through drugs, drink or unhealthy relationships has been self-imposed. In our own lives, they include people who have survived everyday, but still potentially devastating, events such as an unhappy childhood, job loss, separation, divorce, or illness.

> Survivors are people who, in times of crisis or challenge, are able to:
>
> - surmount their troubles by dint of their own efforts
>
> - discover strengths and abilities they didn't previously possess
>
> - gain something of lasting value from their experiences

Would you like to become a survivor? You can by learning to tap into your inborn abilities and turning them into usable skills that you can call on when life gets tough. But first let's see why many of us find survival so hard.

Every baby is born with a healthy instinct for survival. Newborns possess a set of inborn actions, or reflexes, designed to help them to meet their needs. As a baby you knew how to suck and 'root' for your mother's breast or a bottle. Your fingers — and toes — knew how to grip so you could cling on to your mother. And, if you were frightened or surprised, you flung your limbs wide then slowly wrapped them across your body to protect yourself from danger. You cried when you were in pain or distress, calling for those who could ease your pain; you smiled when you were happy, creating a bond of intimacy with those around you. Unfortunately, many of us lose touch with our survival instincts as we grow older. Many of us lose sight of our own identity by trying too hard to please our parents and teachers and be 'good' boys or girls. Some, often those whose parents are struggling for their own survival because of poverty, illness, emotional pain or simply because they are too busy or distracted, start actively doing things to damage themselves. They stress their bodies with junk food; eat too much — or too little; drink or smoke too much; work too hard — or not hard enough; spend too much; or enter relationships that are bad for them. As a result, even everyday life becomes a struggle. If trouble then strikes, it can be extremely difficult to survive.

Some people seem to be born survivors, natural athletes in the game of life. However, all of us can develop survival skills. This book contains clear, strong, simple — and effective — suggestions for doing just that. In it you will learn how to tap into your feelings, make use of the power of your mind, listen to your body and form the strong relationships you need to cope with unwelcome change and crisis.

Part One is all about increasing your personal power to survive, your resilience. In the next chapter we will look at what makes a survivor: the key qualities you need to survive and a basic action plan for dealing with change and stress. In Chapter Two, you will learn how to tune into the messages your body is sending you, how to beat damaging habits and how to look after your body so it can support you in the bad times. In Chapter Three, you will learn the importance of accepting and expressing your feelings, how to deal with your own and other people's feelings and how to transform negative feelings into positive ones. Chapter Four is all about people – a vital strength in times of trouble. In it you will learn how to build relationships with other people so you have a strong support network that is there when you need it. You will learn how to tune into other people, prepare for problems, and deal with them when they arise. In Chapter Five, you will learn about the power of your mind, how to think positively about yourself and how to prevent the way you think from making bad things worse. You will learn the importance of self-esteem, how to lower your defences and how to beat the barriers that may be preventing you from surviving. Finally, in Chapter Six, you will find out about the importance of time and how to anticipate the changes that may occur as you go through life, so you can prepare for them. And you will learn how to put your past behind you.

In Part Two you will learn how to deal with specific challenges in key areas of your life. In Chapter Seven, you will learn all about how to survive the loss of a relationship through separation or divorce. In Chapter Eight you will learn how to survive losing your job, whether you are dismissed or made redundant. Chapter Nine focusses on how to survive illness, whether it is temporary, chronic, progressive or even terminal. Chapter Ten looks at how to survive when the worst really does happen, how to deal with bereavement, losing a partner or child, and how to cope if you have been abused as a child. Chapter Eleven looks towards the future; in it, you will find out what you can do if you are a parent to bring up your children to be survivors, you will learn about how to be a survivor at work, in your close relationships and friendships, and you will also learn what it means to be a survivor both now and in the future. Part Three of the book contains accounts of real-life survivors and examines what qualities they had or developed that enabled them to survive. Use it to gain confidence, courage and inspiration for those times when you need to survive.

Now you have read what *The Survivor Personality* is all about, consider whether you would like to know how to:

- regain your emotional balance when your life is knocked off course?
- maintain your self-confidence in the face of change?
- break free from unhelpful messages from your past?
- choose the right direction when your life reaches a turning point?

Yes? Then let's get started. In the next chapter, we will take a look at the qualities you need to develop a survivor personality.

PART ONE
PERSONAL POWER

CHAPTER ONE
WHAT MAKES A SURVIVOR?

Throughout my life, both in my own existence and in my work as a journalist and writer, I was always interested in what it was that enabled some people to emerge seemingly unscathed from pain and disaster, while others seemed to buckle at the first hint of adversity. In the past few years, psychologists have been looking at just this question. Intriguingly, they have discovered that certain attributes crop up time and again in people who have survived difficult circumstances. Studies of people from all walks of life who have endured difficult and sometimes extreme situations – holocaust survivors, hostages, survivors of major disasters, as well as those who have survived difficult childhoods – have now revealed that those who manage to survive with few or no lasting scars all share a remarkable ability to regain their balance when something goes wrong. This self-righting ability, which psychologists call resilience, is the essence of the survivor personality. The following list, distilled from various different studies, sums up the key qualities.

10 keys to survival

1. High self-esteem – in other words, thinking well of yourself

2. The ability to take responsibility for your feelings and emotions but not to blame yourself when things go wrong

3. The presence of one or more people who believe in you and support you

4. The ability to get on with other people and tune into their feelings

5. The ability to trust in and rely on yourself

6. The confidence to believe that you are in charge of your own life

7. The ability to focus on problems or situations and find ways of dealing with them

8. The ability to be aware of different ways of feeling, thinking about or handling difficult situations

9. A strong personal philosophy

10. A sense of humour

Time and again, it has been found that these qualities give survivors the ability to pick themselves up from whatever life throws at them, learn from it – and then move on. The good news is that all of us, no matter what experiences we have had in our lives until now, can develop resilience. Before you learn more about how to do this, check to see how you are doing so far in the survival stakes. The following checklist is based on scales of resilience devised by psychologists.

Are you a survivor?

Tick the statements that apply to you:

Who are you?

- I'm a planner

- I'm a coper
- I'm a problem-solver
- I'm a juggler (I can deal with many things at once)

What are your strengths?
- I trust in myself more than anybody else
- I am curious
- I can usually see different ways of looking at a situation
- I am my own best friend
- I am determined
- I am self-disciplined (sometimes I force myself to do things whether I want to or not)
- I am able to be alone if I have to be

How do you get through the hard times?
- My past experiences help me deal with difficulties
- My belief in myself sees me through
- I can usually find something to laugh about
- I take things a day at a time
- I have other people I can turn to for support
- I can usually find a way to solve a problem

What are your beliefs?
- It's not my fault when bad things happen
- The way I deal with things that happen is under my control

> - People can rely on me in times of trouble
> - I have the energy to do what I have to do
> - It doesn't matter if some people don't like me
> - I rarely wonder what the point of it all is
> - I feel my life has meaning
> - I feel my life has been a success

How did you get on? If you ticked lots of boxes you already have a pretty good portfolio of resilient attributes that you can call on when life gets tough. If you didn't put down many ticks, don't despair. You decided you were going to become a survivor when you picked up this book. From now on, you are going to learn how to find the resources you need to enable you to survive better in the future. The best news of all is that you don't have to become a different person to become a survivor. The resources you need are already there within you – all you have to do is learn to tap into them and make use of them.

SURVIVAL AND STRESS

To live is to change. However, all change – whether it is good or bad – can cause stress. Stress is a result of being afraid that we won't be able to cope with things that happen. Some years ago, when people first started to study stress, they focussed on big events like getting married or moving in with a partner, having a baby, crashing the car, having to have an operation or getting a divorce. Have a look at the following list, based on one originally developed by two US psychologists, and see how you score.

> Tick the events that have happened to you in the last year:
>
> - My husband/wife/partner has died

- Divorce or separation
- A member of my close family has died
- I have been injured or suffered health problems
- I have lost my job
- I have got back together with a partner I had split up with
- I have retired
- I have been pregnant
- A member of my close family has developed health problems
- I have had sex problems
- I have had a baby
- My business has taken a downward turn
- My financial state has changed for the worse
- A close friend has died
- I have changed my job
- I have had more/less arguments with my partner
- I have taken out a large mortgage or loan
- My work responsibilities have changed
- My children have left home
- I have had trouble with my partner's parents
- I have reached a major goal or made an outstanding personal achievement
- My partner has begun work or lost his/her job
- I have started or finished college or university

- I have moved house or apartment or changed my living set-up
- I have had trouble with my boss
- My working hours or conditions have changed
- I have changed courses or swapped educational establishment
- I have taken up a new hobby or changed the things I do in my spare time
- I have taken out a medium mortgage or loan
- My sleeping pattern has changed (e.g. sleeping more/less, insomnia)
- I am seeing more/less of my family than before
- I have been away on holiday

How did you get on? If you ticked many statements, especially if they came towards the top of the list, you'll be in no doubt that you have been under a lot of potential stress over the last year. In fact, it's not what happens to you that is the most important factor in survival, so much as the way you look at it. For example, if you have been given a promotion, do you see it as a challenge to be greeted with enthusiasm and a sign that your abilities have been recognised? Or do you see it as a terrible burden and feel full of anxiety about your ability to cope? You have a choice.

The way we think, our personal squint on life, plays a large part in the way we feel and the way we act. Approaching life's challenges in a positive, confident frame of mind and with a portfolio of skills to draw on that fit in with your own way of doing things is the key to survival. The good news is that the techniques to change the way you look at life, and by so doing increase your ability to survive whatever it throws at you, lie within everyone's grasp. In the following chapters, you will learn how to think flexibly, how to take charge of your life and how to take active steps to deal with any challenges you might face.

STEELING YOURSELF AGAINST LIFE'S KNOCKS

One of the most important discoveries psychologists have made is that survivors don't acquire the ability to bounce back from adversity by having only good experiences or by avoiding the bad times. In fact, exactly the opposite is the case: it is by being exposed to problems and stresses and coping with them successfully that we build resilience.

The process of enduring life's knocks and gaining strength from them has been described as 'steeling'. It's very similar to the way the body builds immunity to physical infection. Being exposed to illness, whether by catching it or by being immunised, triggers the body to produce antibodies, the immune troops, which fight off infection. The next time you encounter those germs or illness your body's natural defences swing into action. British psychiatrist Professor Michael Rutter, one of the world's leading experts on resilience, believes that our minds have a similar self-protective mechanism. He says, 'Resilience results from having the encounter at a time, and in a way, that the body can cope successfully with the noxious challenge to its system.'

PUTTING THE PAST BEHIND YOU

A key factor in developing physical immunity is being exposed to infection at a time and in such a way that your body is able to fight back. If your body is at a low ebb, because you are very young, very old or your immune system is damaged, then your body finds it harder to protect you. However, by building a strong immune system you can strengthen your body so it is able to protect you better – even though you may need to bear in mind that you have a weakness in a particular area.

The same principle applies to emotional resilience. As Dr M. Scott Peck says in the bestseller, *The Road Less Travelled*,

- *'It is in (the) process of meeting and solving problems that life has its meaning... Problems call forth our courage and our wisdom; indeed they create our courage and our wisdom. It is only because of problems that we grow mentally and spiritually.'*

To cope successfully with adversity you need a strong emotional immune system – and that is what this book is all about. By developing resilience you can both strengthen yourself and buffer yourself against adversity. In this way, you can deprive your past emotional injuries of the power to hurt you. So, even if in the past you have experienced emotional pain that you weren't able to resist at the time, you can now gain the strength to deal with future problems.

HAVE PLAN – WILL COPE WITH CHANGE

As with physical injury, if you bear emotional scars you have to bear them in mind and take steps to protect yourself in order to survive. Research has shown that the way survivors do this is to become great planners. It's long been known that the things we are able to prepare for in advance, such as retirement, are much less stressful than things that we haven't been able to anticipate, such as redundancy. The more you can plan for life's challenges, the better your chance of surviving them. Developing your intuition (see Chapter Three), so your internal radar gives you some advance warning of what lies ahead, is a key survival skill, and one that is vital in planning for change. Although change may seem to happen out of the blue, it is in fact a process with several clear stages. John Norcross, professor of psychology at the University of Scranton in Pennsylvania, USA, has identified five of these.

Underawareness or denial
Thinking about your options

> Preparation
>
> Action
>
> Maintaining the change

STAGE ONE: BEFORE THE FALL

At this stage you are unaware or 'underaware' of a particular problem or you may even deny it altogether. You may know or feel that you are unhappy but be unable to identify the source of your unhappiness. You may begin to ponder the possibility that a particular aspect of your life – your work, your relationship, your health or whatever – is not working. Alternatively, you may deny that something is wrong. For example, you may ignore suspicious bodily symptoms and refuse to go to the doctor, you may refuse to believe that your partner is having an affair, or you may block out the signs that you are about to be given the sack.

STAGE TWO: THINKING ABOUT IT

In this stage, denial stops and your awareness of the problem increases. If you are in an unhappy relationship, you may acknowledge that your partner's infidelity is part of your unhappiness and begin to think about separation. If you have a health problem, you begin to acknowledge the problems and think about making an appointment to see the doctor. If you have a problem at work you may think about what you can do about it.

STAGE THREE: PREPARATION

Now you begin to take small steps towards change. You start to read books about relationships and affairs, you ask friends who have gone through separation how they managed, or you look in the Yellow Pages for the names of solicitors; for health problems, you may look up your symptoms in a health encyclopaedia, 'phone up a support group, ask a friend who had similar symptoms; at work, you ask your colleagues for information that can help you decide whether the threat of getting the sack is real or imagined.

STAGE FOUR: ACTION

In this stage, you begin to take even bigger steps. If you have an unhappy marriage, you go to see a solicitor or insist that your partner goes with you for some counselling. If you have a health problem, you make an appointment to see the doctor. If you are facing the sack or redundancy, you may work in different ways, take on more work or make an appointment to see the boss.

STAGE FIVE: MAINTAINING YOUR GAINS

Finally, you start to reap the benefits of your actions. However, a little upkeep is necessary. So if you have relationship problems you may insist that your partner keeps on with the counselling, even if he swears he will never be unfaithful to you again, or you continue to seek divorce. If you have a health problem, you may have to go for tests, take some medication or change your lifestyle in some way if you are to feel better. At work, you may have to keep working in the new way, or if the discussion with the boss has revealed that you are indeed in line for the sack, you will need to plan further action to enable you to cope.

THE CYCLE OF CHANGE

If you don't manage to make a desired change the first time round, it's important not to regard yourself as a failure. Research has shown that many of us go through the stages of change several times before making a change for good. Just knowing this can improve your odds of dealing successfully with change in the long term. The belief that you can handle things that happen makes you more likely to try for what you want, because you know that if things don't work out you will still gain something useful.

SURVIVING DAILY HASSLES

Knowing how to cope with change, then, is an important part of the survivor's toolkit. However, psychologists have recently discovered that the major events in our lives are actually less stressful than life's everyday hassles. These include annoyances that range from constantly forgetting where you have put your keys, to being trapped in an unhappy relationship or worrying about how you are going to pay the gas bill. In fact, they have found that the amount of measurable stress can actually be predicted more accurately by the number of daily hassles we face than by the number of major events we have experienced. As US psychologist Morton Lieberman puts it, 'We are done in more by the drips than by the floods.'

The key to surviving such everyday nuisances and another important part of the survivor personality is the ability to be flexible. Being flexible doesn't mean always bowing to circumstances, though it can sometimes. What it does mean is being able to choose how you react to situations rather than being dominated by habit. This act of choice puts you more in charge of your life – and this, of course, is one of the biggest keys to survival. Now it's time to check how flexible you are. You will need a pen and notebook.

Have a look at the following list and tick the ones that apply to you. Add any others that you feel are important:

- I am sensitive
- I am strong
- I am a coward
- I am mature
- I am humorous
- I am remote
- I am self-confident
- I am trusting
- I am tough
- I am gentle
- I have courage
- I am childlike
- I am serious
- I am friendly
- I am self-critical
- I am cautious

- I am dependent
- I am impulsive
- I am happy
- I work well with others
- I am proud
- I am selfish
- I am involved
- I am lazy
- I am logical
- I am calm
- I am shy
- I am loving
- I am consistent
- I am messy
- I am optimistic
- I am. . . .
- I am. . . .

- I am independent
- I am well organised
- I am discontented
- I am rebellious
- I am modest
- I am unselfish
- I am detached
- I am hard-working
- I am creative
- I am emotional
- I am outgoing
- I am angry
- I am unpredictable
- I am tidy
- I am pessimistic
- I am. . . .
- I am. . . .

The more pairs of qualities you have ticked the more flexible you are, the bigger the range of choices you have when trouble strikes, and the more successfully you will be able cope in any situation. If you have only ticked a few pairs and more single characteristics, you have less control over how you behave. This means you have to rely more on outside rules and regulations as sources of control. So the workaholic who spends all day – and night – at his desk is just as rigid in his own way as the party animal, who sees working as an unpleasant distraction from parties, dates, holidays and socialising.

Both are less likely to survive than the person who allows time for work and play, and gives them both due importance.

DARE TO BE DIFFERENT

Fortunately, even if you haven't ticked many pairs, now you know what qualities you need to develop and can go ahead and do so. For example, if you dislike conflict and always seek out a quiet life you need to learn to be more direct and confrontational. If you are normally forceful and competitive you need to learn to be more yielding and conciliatory. You will learn more about how to do this in the following chapters. For now, simply become aware of the way you usually behave and next time you face a situation where you are tempted to react in your usual manner, try something different. Don't worry if you find this difficult. Many of us have absorbed the message as children that it's wrong to be flexible. For example, 'You should stick to your guns,' 'Only weak people change their minds,' 'But you always used to love . . .' It isn't easy to change these inner messages and it takes courage. But you can do it. Give yourself time and you will gradually become able to react in more flexible ways. To see how comfortable you feel with being flexible, answer the following questions:

- As a child were you allowed to change your thoughts, feelings or behaviour?
- Were you taught that there was only one way to think, act or feel?
- What happened if you had inconsistent feelings or thoughts?
- How do you feel when someone you know changes their mind, their feelings or their actions?

Don't forget we're not talking here about simply changing your mind for the sake of it. Never knowing what you are going to think, feel or do from one day to the next is a waste of your own energy and makes you a drain on other people. What we are talking about is looking at a situation, assessing it for what it is, and then choosing your response.

HAVING A FULL LIFE

Another of the secrets survivors share, which is linked to being flexible, is the knowledge that a full life is a happy life. If you concentrate on one part of your life to the exclusion of the rest, your life will seem empty if something happens to upset that part and it will be harder to survive. For example, the high-powered businessman or woman whose job is everything is devastated if he or she is made redundant or forced to retire; the parent who has built his or her world around his or her children feels life is meaningless when they leave home; the person whose relationship allows no time for other friends or activities is poleaxed when their partner walks out.

LOOKING AT YOUR WHEEL OF LIFE

To see what this means try the following exercise. You will need a pen, some paper and eight coloured pencils.

> Draw three large circles.
>
> 1. Take the first circle and divide it into eight equal segments like an orange. Colour each segment a different colour and write in the following labels: my spare time; my hobby; my family; my friends; my partner; my work; time spent on my own; time spent on my personal philosophy. This is what your wheel of life looks like if you have a full life.
>
> 2. Now go to the second circle, colour it the appropriate colour and write in just one label from the list,

say 'My work' or 'My partner'. This is what your wheel of life looks like if your work or your partner dominates your life.

3. Now go back to your first wheel and imagine you have lost your job or your relationship has broken up. Colour that segment in black.

4. Now do the same with the second wheel and compare the two. Unless you are exceptionally unlucky, most changes tend to affect just one or two areas of your life, so having a full life means that if something goes wrong in one area of your life, there are plenty of joys in the other parts to help you to survive. If your wheel of life revolves around just one aspect, it's hardly surprising that the wheel collapses if you lose that thing.

5. Now go to the third circle and draw the segments in your wheel of life. Are there any that are missing, any that don't have enough space, or any that have too much? What would happen to you if those areas fell apart? Now think about what you can do about it.

CRISIS AND SURVIVAL

A crisis is, by its nature, unexpected. It is an event, situation or experience that happens suddenly and has repercussions in every area of your life. It has lots in common with change, except that because it often strikes suddenly, you usually have less time to prepare. Even so, some crises do build gradually. Being aware of what is going on in your life, by learning to listen to your body, tuning in to your own and other people's feelings, and knowing what challenges you are likely to encounter at various times in your life, can help you to prepare.

The word crisis in Chinese has two meanings, 'danger' and 'opportunity'. True to their ability to be flexible, survivors usually keep both meanings in mind when reacting to crisis. At first you may feel immobilised: numb, out of control and unable to act. After this, crisis tends to follow a similar course to change. You may minimise the problem, describe it as trivial or deny it. You may then undergo a period of self-doubt and depression as reality sinks in. This low point is followed by acceptance and letting go, as the reality of your situation hits home. At this point, your self-esteem often rises again as you think of ways you can deal with the situation and begin to make sense of it.

Crisis management involves first of all damage limitation – dealing with the immediate problems a crisis throws up as best you can. The next step is to think about what is likely to happen next, and devise an action plan for dealing with this. After the crisis, you may be able to look back and see how it came to happen, so you will be more able to cope next time. You may also be able to see something good in the crisis, even if it seemed entirely negative at the time. You'll learn more about how to sense impending crises as you read Part One. In Part Two, you'll find hints on how to deal with some specific crises. Now let's look at one of the most effective skills survivors bring into play when dealing with any sort of change or crisis.

LEARNING FROM EXPERIENCE

People with a non-survival approach towards life are prone to dwell on unpleasant things that have happened to them. Sometimes this is because of a superstitious fear that by letting go they will bring down the wrath of the gods. At other times, it may be because they are afraid that if they concentrate on the good things that happen they are bound to fail. Sometimes, it could be that negative attitudes blind them to positive changes. Finally, they may be guilty of staying in 'victim mode' to gain attention. Getting bogged down in unpleasant past experiences without learning from them leaves you open to being victimised again the next time a similar situation occurs.

Survivors, on the other hand, are constantly learning from their experiences. To see how you develop this skill try the following exercise. You will need a pen, a notebook and some time.

> Now think about something bad that happened to you in the past – a divorce or a distressing break up – and do the following:
>
> 1. Re-live the experience. Rerun it in your mind like a video. Just watch it: don't try to explain it in ways that justify or condemn what happened.
>
> 2. Describe the experience. Talk about it to a friend, write about it in your diary, paint a picture, or write a poem about it.
>
> 3. Ask yourself what you learned from the experience. If it happened again, what would you do next time?
>
> 4. Imagine yourself talking or acting in a more effective way next time.
>
> 5. Mentally rehearse doing it in the way you desire.

How did you get on? Are you feeling stronger? By re-living experiences you have had in the past, you learn a lot about yourself. You can track back to early clues you ignored and decide what to do – or not to do – next time. By learning to process experiences this way, you will gain self-confidence for handling similar situations better in future.

THE SURVIVOR SEQUENCE

Now you know something about the nature of change and crisis, you are ready to learn about what you can do in the face of them to survive. When faced with any sort of challenge, survivors are quick to engage in the survivor sequence. First of all, you must regain your emotional balance by learning to control or express your feelings. Secondly, you must adapt and cope with the immediate situation. This involves taking care of yourself mentally and physically so you don't expose yourself to undue extra stress. Thirdly, you must learn to thrive. This means being able to anticipate and plan for what happens next. It may also involve learning to think, feel and act in new ways and becoming more open and creative in the way you deal with problems. Finally, you must allow yourself to find the gift, the good thing that you have gained from your bitter experience. If you put these steps into practice whenever bad times come your way, you will gain another attribute of the survivor personality: the ability to convert disaster into good fortune.

WHAT MAKES A SURVIVOR? ROUNDUP

When putting the survivor sequence into practice, bear in mind that any change takes time, and be prepared to take it slowly, taking small steps. It's always easier to stay the same than to change, so don't be hard on yourself if you find it hard to move forward when you encounter setbacks. Remember that change is a process, not a once and for all event. To help keep up your motivation to change, check out the following benefits of developing a survivor personality.

Developing survival skills will enable me to:

- Look forward to the future with positive anticipation
- Become more self-confident and willing to take risks
- Try out some of the strategies that have worked for other survivors and see how well they work for me
- Learn more and more as I go through life
- Create my own solutions to problems and ways of doing things without having to wait for other people

Convinced? Then you are ready for the next step, learning to tune into the wisdom of your body, so that it works for you and not against you.

CHAPTER TWO
BODY POWER

A key aspect of the survivor personality is intuition, sometimes described as 'knowledge gained without rational thought'. Intuition means being alert to messages coming from your subconscious mind. The world reaches your mind through your body. Learning to respect your body, to listen to and understand its language, is a vital survival skill. Increased sensitivity to your physical sensations enables you to gain access to your body's knowledge, allowing you to let go of past pains and develop the intuition you need to deal with whatever life throws at you.

LISTENING TO YOUR BODY

As a newborn baby, you had no trouble in listening to your body and letting it protect you. There was no boundary between your body and that of your mother or the person caring for you – at least in your mind. All the physical sensations you experienced – warmth or cold, dryness or moisture, satisfaction or hunger, the loving touch of someone who cared for you or lack of touch – were part of you in your mind. If your parents were sensitive to your bodily needs and satisfied them you will have begun to trust your body and develop a positive attitude towards it. If when you cried with hunger, you were fed, when you cried with cold, you were wrapped in a warm blanket, you learnt that your needs could be met. At the same time you developed a bond with those who cared for you. And gradually, as you came to realise that you had a separate body – around six or seven months of age – that bond became stronger. If your parents were inexperienced or neglectful, you may have learnt to distrust or ignore the messages your body sends you. One of the most important things you learn as a survivor is how to get back in touch with your bodily sensations and what they mean.

TUNING IN TO YOUR BODY'S LANGUAGE

All our perceptions of the world are filtered through our senses: what we see, hear, touch, taste and smell. When we *feel* an emotion we feel it in our bodies. When you are afraid you may notice a sinking feeling in your stomach, a tightening of the chest, a dry mouth, or a feeling that you can't breathe. If you feel happy your chest expands, your face relaxes, your heart literally feels light as you breathe more easily and the blood flows around your body more freely.

As a first step to learning to listen to your body, think back to a time when something good happened to you, whether it was hearing that you had passed an important exam, buying a new piece of furniture for your sitting-room, being proposed to by your partner, or signing a business deal. Now try to remember the physical sensations that accompanied your feelings: the sigh that went with your relief, the tingle of excitement that went down your spine, the warmth of satisfaction. These sensations may have only lasted for a brief moment, but rest assured they were there.

Now think back to a time when something bad happened to you: when you scanned the exam list and realised you had failed, when you splashed out on a new piece of furniture with money you hadn't got, when the proposal from your partner was that you split up, when the business deal failed to materialise. Again think back to what you felt in your body: a sinking feeling in your stomach that signalled anxiety, a clenching in your chest that signalled fear, sighing that signalled disappointment or sadness, the nervous way you cleared your throat which signalled your shyness. These are your body's alarm bells and you ignore them at your peril.

WHAT IS YOUR BODY TRYING TO TELL YOU?

The language of your body often mirrors the language of your mind. However, sometimes no matter how hard our bodies are trying to tell us something, we don't take any notice of its language. We ignore the signals we are getting or force ourselves to override them, often because of messages from our past about what we 'should' or 'ought' to do. When this happens the initial signals may seem to disappear. However, your body keeps shouting louder and louder, trying to alert you. You may develop physical discomforts such as headaches, indigestion, loss of appetite, aches and pains in your muscles, or diarrhoea. Psychologists have discovered that emotional pain can become 'locked' in our bodies. The way you hold yourself, the way you breathe, and your facial expression all provide important clues about you, your feelings and the way you approach life. With each emotional knock we may 'armour' ourselves physically as well as emotionally against bad feelings. Physical complaints such as backache, stiff neck, tight chest, headaches and migraines, even chronic complaints like asthma, can all have their roots in feelings, which we have held back or not expressed.

As time goes on, you may continue to ignore your body's shouts for attention, trying to drown them out with compulsive eating, drinking, smoking, prescribed or non-prescribed drugs or other harmful physical addictions. In the short term these may help, but in the long term they can damage your ability to survive.

TREATING YOUR BODY BETTER

A first step in learning to trust the wisdom of your body is to start treating it better. And one of the most important ways you can do that is to start thinking about what you put in it. What you eat, drink or smoke affects the way you think and the amount of energy you have available for survival. Making sure you eat the right foods and drop harmful habits is vital for survival.

EAT TO SURVIVE

We need proper nutrients to protect ourselves from disease and to keep us in tip-top health so we have the energy we need in times of trouble to survive. The following three-point plan will help you survive with food:

> 1. Aim to eat several small meals a day rather than one big meal. What you eat and when you eat it can affect your mental and physical energy. Nutritionists have discovered that the old adage, 'Breakfast like a king, lunch like a prince and dine like a pauper' makes good sense. Eating late at night stresses the digestive system, makes it more difficult to sleep, and lays down fat, because you are creating excess physical energy at a time when your body needs it least.
>
> 2. Keep a balance in your eating habits. How much you eat also affects your capacity to survive. If you constantly eat too much, the extra pounds you are shipping can deplete the mental and physical energy you need for survival. If you find that difficult to believe, think about how sluggish you feel after a big dinner. On the other hand, if you eat too little, you starve your body and mind, depriving it of the energy to survive. People with anorexia pour all their energy into staying thin, rather than surviving.
>
> 3. Think about the value of what you eat. In recent years, nutritionists have pinpointed the existence of certain 'superfoods'. These are foods rich in the vitamins and

> minerals that are vital for bodily survival. In particular, vitamins C, E and beta-carotene, together with the mineral selenium – all found in fruit and vegetables – have been found to protect the body against ageing and life-threatening diseases such as heart disease and cancer, and other chronic conditions that affect the quality of life such as diabetes and cataracts. So if you want to survive to a ripe old age, it pays to follow the advice of nutritionists and aim to eat at least five helpings of fruit and vegetables a day and consider taking a multi-vitamin and mineral supplement.

EXERCISE TO SURVIVE

Exercise is also vital if you want to survive. Exercise helps you to build up strength, mobility and stamina – all vital when you are facing challenges, whether they are mental or physical. Exercise also makes you look and feel better – important for confidence – helps keep your weight under control, helps you sleep better, eat better and feel less depressed. It tones up your muscles, strengthens your bones and raises levels of endorphins (hormone-like substances that help us to endure mental and physical pain and produce feelings of well-being). Convinced? Then why not start today?

Have a think about what exercises or activities you might enjoy doing and then develop an action plan (for tips on developing action plans see the companion to this book, *How To Get What You Want*) to make sure you put it into practice.

Swedish exercise physiologist Dr Gunnar Borg has discovered that we each have a highly accurate internal barometer which tells us whether we are exercising to the right intensity for us. Aim to work at a level which you find challenging but not so hard that you are uncomfortable. Monitor your pulse (you can find out how in any good exercise book, or from the trainer at your gym or exercise class). Your exercising heart rate should be between 120 and 170 beats per minute.

Jane Fonda's famous 'burn' is a sign of lactic acid building up in your muscles as a result of using energy. Provided it goes away when you stop exercising, it is normal muscle fatigue. Simply stop, relax your muscles for a few minutes, and continue if necessary. The fitter you are, the longer you can keep going without getting the burn.

If you find yourself feeling weak or tired, it is a sign that you are tired, dehydrated or running low on energy stores, or that you are over-exercising. Injury is more likely if you are overtired, so stop and rest. Make sure you drink plenty of water or a fitness drink, before, during and after working out.

Here are some more exercise tips:

- Be realistic. Work out how much time you can afford — aim for a minimum of 30 minutes three times a week — and then find something you can do in that time.

- Try to incorporate more activity into your everyday life. Leave the car at home, walk up stairs rather than taking a lift and so on.

- Always spend time warming up and cooling down.

- Find out as much as you can about particular exercises and activities and the benefits they confer. Then try to devise a balanced programme that gives you strength, flexibility and stamina.

- If you develop physical symptoms such as ulcers, sore throats, insomnia or fatigue, you could be overdoing it. Stay in touch with your body and know when it has had enough.

RELAX TO SURVIVE

Relaxation is as vital as activity to survival — remember what we said about adaptability? It's as important to know when to stop as it is to keep going. Everyday activities such as making your bed, washing up, or sweeping the floor can help you to relax, by calming your mind. When you perform such tasks, become aware of your body and the muscles you are using: the stretch in your back when bending to make the bed, the way you stand when you sweep the floor, the strength in your buttocks as you pick up a child, the stretch in your arms as you put something on a high shelf, the feel of your body as you walk upstairs.

Learning to relax means being aware of when your body needs to stop and take a break. Busy people often find it difficult or impossible to slow down when there is a lull in their daily activity. However, by not doing so you are putting yourself on the road to burn-out – or non-survival. Taking a short time to stop and let go helps you clear your mind and lifts stress and tension, so you are able to harness your energy more effectively for survival.

Survivor tips for busy people

1. Take ten

All you need is ten seconds to calm your mind before and after finishing something you are doing. Try to take ten regularly throughout your day:

- Breathe in slowly and deeply from your abdomen for a count of five

- Place your feet firmly on the floor and be aware of them connecting with the floor

- Breathe out slowly to a count of five, become aware of your breath leaving your lungs and passing out through your air passages. Be aware of the stretch in your spine that happened as you breathed in

- Breathe naturally again and go on to the next thing you have to do

2. Take five

Just five minutes can rest and restore your muscles. You can take five wherever you are – at home or work, when you are travelling, when you have to wait for an appointment or during coffee or tea breaks.

- Sit, feet flat on the floor, knees a comfortable distance apart, hands loosely in your lap. The base of your spine should be in contact with the back of your chair, your back upright and your head balanced, and your eyelids lightly closed

- Breathe slowly and deeply in from your abdomen, then breathe slowly out

- Focus your attention on each part of your body in turn, paying especial attention to your head and your hands. Become aware of each part of your body and feel it becoming warm, loose, soft and relaxed. Start with the back of your head and work gradually over the top of your head and scalp, forehead, eyes and face. Let your jaw relax and your tongue rest loosely touching the back of your lower, front teeth. Feel your throat, neck, shoulders becoming relaxed and loose; your shoulders, arms, hands; your back, abdomen, pelvis, buttocks, legs and feet.

- Take another slow deep breath in – and out. Stretch your hands, arms, legs and feet and feel the energy returning into them

- Now open your eyes and get on with what you have to do next

3. Take 20

Twenty to thirty minutes is all you need to get really relaxed. Try to relax really deeply at least once a day.

> There are various techniques you can use and you might find it useful to invest in a relaxation tape. Here's one I find useful.
>
> - Choose a time when you know you won't be interrupted. Unplug the phone, close the door
>
> - Loosen any tight clothing and lie down flat on the floor. If your back is not comfortable put a cushion under your knees. Let your body surrender to the floor. Feel each part of your body relax and loosen as you did in the exercise above
>
> - Breathe in and out slowly, concentrating on each breath. If thoughts pop into your mind let them go – imagine they are clouds passing across a blue sky – and return to concentrating on your breathing
>
> - Imagine a favourite scene, for example, lying on a warm beach. Feel the warm sand beneath your body, soft and just slightly gritty, feel the sun gently warming and relaxing your face, cheeks, neck and body. You are completely relaxed, with the sun warming you and your mind at rest

With practice you will be able to relax easily any time you want.

AVOIDING THE BODY BREAKERS

Some of the things we put into our bodies actively damage our capacity to survive. For instance if you are hooked on coffee, tea or cola-type drinks you over-stimulate your body and your mind. Too much caffeine boosts anxiety and the resulting arousal can make it hard to think clearly and focus on what you need to do when bad times arise. Smoking is also linked to lack of mental and physical energy – as well as being damaging to your long-term health and survival. Studies have shown that smokers are twice as likely to report feelings of tiredness as non-smokers. Unfortunately, an all too common reaction to this is to light up another cigarette, and so it goes on. Alcohol, too, though a small amount can be protective, can deprive us of mental and physical energy. One of its most insidious qualities is that it appears to relax us, by acting as a short-term sedative. However, after a few hours it stimulates the brain, causing insomnia and anxiety. Too much alcohol is also linked to shortages of vital nutrients.

BEATING THE BODY BREAKERS

Ridding yourself of a bad habit such as smoking, overeating or drinking to excess is very different from changing your career or breaking up with your partner. For a start, you need to understand what drives you to smoke, overeat or whatever.

If you smoke, for example, you need to find out what needs a cigarette fills, as well as quelling the urge for nicotine. Is your lighting up part of a comfortable ritual, such as drinking your morning coffee or tea, or chatting with friends after dinner? Do you do it to relieve stress? Or as a safety valve to help you calm down and rid yourself of tension?

There are plenty of reasons to ditch a bad habit, even it's just to improve the image you project. Give up smoking, for example, and other people no longer view you as an addict; stop overeating and people alter their view of you. But for perseverance to stick to your resolution, you must first understand what provokes your habit.

So you've made up your mind. You've decided you want to beat your bad habit, but it's often easier said than done. The following ten tips can help get you started

- Eat more fresh fruit and vegetables . . . and then do it
  Fresh fruit and vegetables make the body more alkaline, so it expels chemicals more slowly, and this in turn extends the time before you need your next 'fix'.

- Take up exercise . . . and then do it
  Exercise releases endorphins, the body's natural feel-good hormones, which give you a sense of well-being that may reduce your craving.
- Join a self-help group . . . and then do it
  The support of others who understand what you are going through and can give mutual support is invaluable – hence the success of stopping smoking groups, and groups such as Alcoholics Anonymous, Narcotics Anonymous and so on.
- Learn to relax . . . and then do it
  Relaxation can reduce stress and tension and allow you to get more in tune with your body. However, on it's own relaxation may not be enough . . .
- Sign up for a course of alternative therapy . . . and then do it
  Hypnosis, acupuncture and a number of other alternative therapies can be useful in supporting your body while you give up a bad habit. However, you must have the motivation too. As one acupuncturist warned me, 'Acupuncture can't help someone to give up whatever it is they are doing if they don't really want to.'
- Find a new routine . . . and then do it
  Take up a new hobby – making jewellery, knitting, painting, visiting galleries, read a book, play with worry beads – anything to distract you from your addiction.
- Avoid people and places which tempt you to indulge your habit . . . and then do it
  Many of us associate our habit with particular people and places. For example, you may always light up after a meal or share a cigarette with a particular friend. You may always have a cream cake when you visit a particular restaurant with your daughter. Just for a little while try avoiding the people and places you associate with your habit. Once you've started to drop your habit, you can explain what you are doing and ask these people for their support in helping you.

- Improve your image . . . and then do it
  If you feel bad about your body, you don't care how you look after it. However, you can turn around the way you feel by improving your image. There are tips on boosting your self-esteem in Chapter Six, but in the first instance, as we're talking about body power, why not think about changing your appearance? There are many choices open to you – clothes, diet and exercise, cosmetics or even cosmetic surgery. (See the companion to this book, *How To Get What You Want*, for more hints on improving your appearance.)
- Go away on holiday . . . and then do it
  Going away on holiday is another way of changing your routine. Away from the stresses and strains of your life you may feel less need to indulge your bad habit. So get down to the travel agent and book that trip of a lifetime.
- See a shrink . . . and then do it
  Most bad habits are linked to the way we live and the way we feel about ourselves. So you need to work out when you feel the need to indulge your habit. Sometimes learning how to view a stressful situation in a new light can help. Cognitive psychotherapy, which helps you think in new ways about things, can often help.

Encouraged? I hope so. In the short term it can be difficult to change your habits, but if you keep at it your determination will grow – and with it your instinct to survive.

BODY POWER ROUNDUP

Now you have become aware of your body and how, if you treat it well and learn to trust it, it can look after you and help you survive. Take some time to think about the present state of your physical self and how you can tune into your body's wisdom about its own needs. Consider what areas need encouragement or further development and what areas need healing. Now check the following list:

- I enjoy my body and how I look
- I intend to take care of my body and my health
- I feel physically competent and strong
- I enjoy feeding my body well
- I can tune into the pleasures of my senses

Yes? Now you are ready to find out about another vital survival skill: being able to tune into your own and other people's feelings and emotions.

CHAPTER THREE
FEELING POWER

The way you cope when bad times come along depends very largely on the emotional repertoire at your disposal and your skill in using it. Think about how, when you are feeling sad, the whole world seems grey and nothing seems worthwhile. On the other hand, when you are feeling happy, the world appears brighter and you feel you can move mountains. Our emotions affect how we perceive what is happening to us, our thoughts and our actions. Being able to identify and express your emotions enables you to harness them and use them to help you get through troubled times. If you can't identify your emotions you will be confused by what is happening to you and feel out of control. If you can't express your emotions you will be isolated and unable to obtain the support you need. If you withold your emotions you may become physically or mentally ill.

TINY TEARS

Our emotions are among the battery of survival skills we are all born with. Our biological clocks are programmed in such a way that all over the world babies show the same basic emotions at exactly the same ages. Our most basic emotion, the one we are all born with, is curiosity: a newborn baby presented with a new face or object will stare at it intently with unmistakable interest. Newborn babies also express pain (by crying) and disgust (by wrinkling their noses). At around three months of age, we gain enough control over our arms and legs to push things that displease us away – we start to express anger. Anyone who has seen a baby of this age in a paroxysm of rage can testify to this. Equally recognisable from the down-turned mouth and wrinkled brow is the three-month-old's sadness. At around five to seven months of age (around the age we begin to realise that we are separate individuals), fear comes onto our emotional stage.

As awareness of our separate identity grows, we begin to develop other emotions: toddlers become noticeably embarrassed if asked to show off in front of strangers. As we grow ever more sophisticated, other emotions pop up. At three years old, pride (smiling, clapping and shouting 'I did it'), guilt (looking down and mumbling '*I* did it') and shame (slumping and saying 'I'm not good at this') make their appearance in our emotional repertoire.

DEVELOPING YOUR EMOTIONAL REPERTOIRE

Survivors are those who have managed to keep in touch with the whole range of their emotions and have developed a portfolio of emotional skills. The degree of comfort we feel expressing our emotions often goes back to childhood. One of the first lessons most of us learn is that positive emotions like joy and curiosity are more welcome than negative ones like sadness and anger.

If, as a child, you were allowed and encouraged to notice and express your emotions, you are likely to feel comfortable with expressing a range of different ones. However, many people's emotional development has been stunted. We learn that it's bad to show our emotions. We are taught that it is wrong to complain or be unhappy. As a result we begin to block our emotions. Blocked emotional energy from the past can hold you back when trouble strikes. The good news is that it's never too late to learn how to extend your emotional skills. Your reward will be less stress, more confidence in yourself and an increased ability to get through the bad times.

Tick the messages you remember from your childhood:

- Don't talk back
- Stop complaining
- Don't cry
- Don't be selfish
- Be polite
- Stop whining
- Stop pouting
- Smile
- Don't ask questions
- Don't be angry

Add any others not listed that you remember.

If you heard any of these messages, you may have learned to think of certain emotions as being bad. To be bad means being punished, spanked, rejected, scolded ... and sent up to your room without any pudding! To get the love and acceptance all children need you may have learnt to suppress your 'bad' emotions. The trouble is that people who were brought up not to be bad are not equipped emotionally to deal with change. To see how the messages you received in your childhood may have handicapped you in dealing with change, think a bit more about some of the following:

- As a child were you encouraged to *acknowledge* your emotions?
  Many parents don't allow their children to feel their true emotions, sometimes because they find them too threatening themselves. If your emotions were ignored, not talked about, or if you were always encouraged to be logical and

reasonable, you may now feel confused and unable to identify your emotions.

- As a child were you allowed to *show* your emotions?

    If you were sad were you allowed to cry? If you were happy were you allowed to show your joy? In some families, expression of emotions is regarded as a bad thing. If you were feeling down you may have been told, 'Come on, cheer up, it's not that bad', 'Give us a smile' or, 'What have you got to be miserable about?' If you were happy you may have heard, 'You can wipe that smile off your face', or 'What have you got to be so pleased about?' Such messages can lead us to be afraid of expressing our emotions openly.

- As a child were you allowed to express the *strength* of your feelings?

    All too often, even if we are allowed to express our emotions, we are not allowed to express them fully. If you were howling with rage you may have been told, 'All right, that's enough, it's time to cut it out.' If you were sobbing with sadness, 'It's not that bad.' If you were feeling happy and boisterous, 'OK, quieten down, you're making too much noise.' As a result, you may feel you have to restrain your emotions.

- As a child were you taught that it is alright to have a wide *range* of emotions?

    Many families have 'good' emotions and 'bad' emotions. 'Good' emotions are things like happiness, joy, pleasure or gratitude, which you are allowed to express. 'Bad' emotions are things like anger, fear, sadness, jealousy and curiosity, which you are not allowed to express or were criticised for. For example, if you showed interest in something you may have been told, 'Don't stare', 'It's rude to be nosy.' An angry frown may have triggered the reaction, 'If the wind changes your face will stay like that'. If you were not allowed to express your true emotions, you may have learnt to hide them behind other more acceptable ones. This can lead to emotional crossed wires and inappropriate behaviour like smiling when you are angry. Alternatively, you may have learnt to deny what you are feeling, for example by saying, 'Oh I'm alright' – when quite clearly you are not.

Many of us spend our whole lives trying to please our parents by being good. The price we pay can be high. We end up, in effect, lying about our emotions. Rather than being emotionally honest, we only express the emotions we believe are acceptable. Have a look at the following and tick any that apply to you:

- I often smile when I am upset
- I usually don't tell other people when I am angry with them
- I feel uncomfortable asking for things for myself
- I often smile and compliment people to their faces but bitch about them behind their backs
- I believe it is my duty to point out other people's faults – for their own good
- I'm not very good at accepting compliments or agreeing that I am good at something
- I'm often afraid that others will see me as hurtful, tough, selfish, insensitive or uncaring

DEVELOPING EMOTIONAL VERSATILITY

Being a survivor involves ditching unhelpful messages from your past and allowing yourself to identify and express the full range of your emotions. Remember there are no such things as 'good' or 'bad' emotions. Your emotions simply are. Some people, having imbibed some of the messages of positive thinking, believe they must be positive on every occasion. In fact, there's absolutely nothing wrong with feeling pessimistic, unhappy or negative when something bad happens. In fact, in recent years psychologists have actually identified a characteristic they describe as 'defensive pessimism' – a belief that the worst is going to happen that prods you into trying to stop it from happening – that actually has survival value. If you're a defensive pessimist you may approach a difficult experience with the fear that you won't be able to cope. This causes you to prepare for the experience and, as a result, when you face it you do cope. You then feel pleasantly surprised: things turned out better than you expected. So 'defensive pessimism' can actually be a survival strategy.

The point is that survivors are versatile emotionally. They are able to judge when it is the right time to express emotions and when they need to control them. Emotional versatility involves being able to draw on the following skills:

- Controlling your emotions
- Being aware of your emotions
- Expressing your emotions
- Letting go of your emotions
- Transforming your emotions

DEVELOPING EMOTIONAL CONTROL

The ability to control your emotions is vital if you are to survive. Our emotions are good servants but tyrannical masters. It's important to recognise that there are occasions when it's preferable to hold back your emotions, for example, when letting it all out may hurt someone unnecessarily, or in times of stress when emotions can get the upper hand. Learning emotional control doesn't mean never showing your emotions; it means being able to judge when it is appropriate to show them and, if necessary, saving them for a time and place when you can discharge them safely.

- Remove yourself from the stressful situation
  Research shows that, especially with anger, it really can help to go out of the room for a few minutes, perform a 'holding' ritual like putting the kettle on, and give yourself time to calm down a little.
- Learn to switch
  You can change your emotional state and gain control over your emotions by learning to switch from one emotion to another. Ways of switching include doing something physically active, moving, looking out of the window, going for a run, thinking about something else, or changing the subject of a conversation by talking about something else or making a joke.
- Focus on the positive
  However small it is, there is usually something positive to be gained from any situation. Try to think about this. For example, if you have been told you are being made redundant, 'At least I won't have to battle with the rush hour every morning.' Even in extreme situations, for instance when someone you love has died, there is always something positive to be gained. This could be anything from meeting other friends of that person and learning something new about the person you loved, to gaining greater understanding of yourself and others through your grief.
- Learn meditation, relaxation or breathing techniques
  Techniques of the sort described in the last chapter can help give you breathing space so you can decide how, where and when it is most appropriate to show your emotions.

DEVELOPING EMOTIONAL AWARENESS

Awareness of how you react when you are feeling angry, sad, happy, afraid, embarrassed and so on is vital. Becoming aware of your emotions and how they feel helps you to take charge so you can choose when and where you need to control your emotions and when and where you can let rip. To develop awareness of your emotions:

- Accept your emotions
  When you have an emotion, try not to suppress it immediately – allow yourself to feel it and express it. You'll find some suggestions below.
- Learn to listen to your body language
  Draw on the skills you learnt in the last chapter and become aware of what your posture, facial expression, or bodily movements are telling you about your emotions.
- Realise that it is possible to feel conflicting emotions
  Don't try to suppress one of your emotions because you feel it is unacceptable. Recognise that you can feel angry and sad (for example, when someone dies), happy and afraid (for example, if you are told you have got a job you very much want), and so on. Don't censor your emotions, simply let them be.
- Learn to recognise how your emotions affect the way you behave
  We are all individuals and each of us reacts differently to different emotions. Start to become aware of how you act when you are feeling a particular emotion. When you are afraid, you may behave nervously, withdraw from other people, run away from the thing you are afraid of, or face out your fear; when you are happy, you may talk a lot, want to celebrate or 'phone all your friends; when you are sad, you may shut yourself away, or may want to have people with you.

Learning about your own emotional style can help you to gain emotional mastery. Once you know how you react, you can start practising different reactions to increase your emotional repertoire.

LEARNING TO EXPRESS YOUR EMOTIONS

Talking about how you feel helps you to trust the people around you and helps them to trust you. Communicating your emotions isn't always easy, because it involves risking other people knowing you as you really are, laying you open to being rejected or hurt. As you practise communicating your emotions, however, you will find that the benefits you gain from more honest, open relationships far outweigh the potential losses.

- Practise talking about how you are feeling
  It isn't always easy to find the words to describe our emotions but it's simply a matter of finding a style you feel comfortable with. If you find it hard to talk about your emotions, you may find it helpful to start noticing how other people do it. Listen to people talking and note how they express their emotions, read poems and note how poets find metaphors for emotions, listen to songs and think about how the singers express their emotions.
- Get used to talking about your feelings in your everyday conversation
  Get into practice by starting to use words to describe pleasant or unpleasant feelings as you go about your daily life. Start with the small things that have made you happy or experience mild irritation, sadness or fear. As you begin to feel more confident, you will feel more comfortable about expressing the emotions that are more difficult for you. Take your time and don't force your pace.
- Share some of your warm emotions with other people
  Get used to saying, 'I like you' and 'I love you', to putting a supportive arm around someone who is unhappy or giving someone you love a hug.
- Ask someone to listen to you
  If you are feeling weak or vulnerable, ask a friend or

relative to listen to you. Explain that you don't expect them to come up with solutions or even to speak, that you just want them to listen. Get used to feeling what it is like to unburden your emotions. Realise that you won't be destroyed by it.

- Learn to express uncomfortable emotions
  Get used to naming your emotions — especially the ones you feel uncomfortable with. If you feel embarrassed about something, say so, before explaining what it is about the situation that has this effect on you. This helps to defuse the emotion and gives it less power. The same goes for anger and other negative emotions.

- Take an interest in other people's emotions
  Encourage other people to express their emotions to you, but don't force them. When we open up to someone else, we usually do so in tandem. You confide in a friend that you're having problems in your relationship. She confides in you that her partner is unfaithful. This mutual exchange makes you feel safe in revealing your emotions. Don't force self-revelation unless you are prepared to reveal your emotions and don't give advice unless someone asks you for it. Learn to accept what others tell you about their emotions, without criticising them just because you would react differently.

LEARNING TO LET GO OF YOUR EMOTIONS

The ability to release emotions, to 'let off steam' is a vital part of the survivor personality. However before you learn how, a couple of rules:
1. Pick your time and place. Remember that it isn't always appropriate to let rip wherever you are or with anyone and everyone.
2. Start gradually. If you are not used to letting off steam emotionally, it can be quite scary, so do so for short periods at first, using the

control and switching methods described below to bring yourself out of it.

Here are a few suggestions for letting go:

For releasing anger:
- Scream, shout into a pillow or out loud (choose somewhere where you won't be overheard)
- Save up broken plates, cups and other crockery and hurl them at a wall or the floor when you are feeling pent up
- Collect cardboard boxes from the supermarket and bash them or kick them
- Use your mattress or pillows as a punchball and hit and punch them when you are feeling angry

For releasing sadness:
- Play sad music
- Draw the curtains
- Write down your thoughts in a diary
- Write a poem or a story, paint a picture, compose some music
- Write a sad letter about the event that is making you sad
- Cry

For releasing joy:
- Shout, laugh, blow up a balloon
- Call a friend
- Plan a celebration
- Make love
- Give yourself a present

TRANSFORMING YOUR EMOTIONS

A vital part of surviving is the ability to harness the energy of your emotions and use it for constructive thought or action. Here are a few suggestions:

- Do something physical to galvanise your energy. For example, if you are worried about something, go for a

swim or a run – and then start doing what you have to do
- Use your feelings to create something – a picture, a poem, a piece of jewellery
- Build up your fitness (see Chapter Two). Then you can work-out, dance, play a hard game of squash or whatever to release pent-up energy when you are under stress
- Learn to meditate. Meditation often helps to change negative emotions into creative ideas.

Transforming fear
- Learn to recognise how cycles of fear build up and break them
- Learn to relax and do so when you approach something you fear
- Work out a step-by-step programme of 'controlled exposure' to the thing you fear
- Reward yourself when you manage to conquer a fear

Transforming anger
- Be open about your feelings
- Think about the underlying reasons for your anger and work at ridding yourself of them (for example when you are angry with your partner for not helping you with the drying-up, is it really him, or your parents you are angry with?)
- Write a letter to the person you are angry with saying exactly what you wished you had said (keep it and then burn it)
- Put your anger away in a mental 'drawer' and close it

Transforming sadness
- Find some support
- Do something active
- Write down negative thoughts and learn to challenge them
- Recognise when your sadness is concealing anger and then work at that
- Be kind to yourself and pat yourself on the back for your achievements

DEVELOPING CONFIDENCE WITH YOUR EMOTIONS

One reason many of us are afraid of expressing our emotions is that they can make us feel uncomfortable physically. You may sob with despair, quake with fear, feel you are going to burst with rage, or feel eaten up inside by jealousy. Because these physical sensations are so intense you may fear that you will never be able to stop them, that you will literally cry for ever, or that you will never be able to control your rage. Learning that you can't be totally swept away by your emotions – that you will stop crying, that the shaking, trembling, dry mouth and breathlessness of fear or panic will subside – can help you to feel more at ease with expressing your emotions. Now try the following exercise:

> 1. The next time you feel sad or unhappy, find yourself some space to be alone in and really get into the feeling. Tell yourself that you are going to enjoy being unhappy. Put on some sad music, dress in black, beat your chest and allow yourself to feel your unhappiness physically. Feel your heart ache, your stomach ache, your eyes stream. Let the feelings wash over you and take as long as you like.
>
> 2. You will notice that after a while the feelings gradually subside and become weaker. As they do so take a long, slow, deep breath in and relax thoroughly (see the last chapter for more details on how). Now give yourself some encouraging messages such as, 'It's going to be alright,' 'I'm OK' and 'I can cope.'
>
> 3. Notice how your sensations and emotions change as you go into this period of calm. You may feel cleansed and refreshed, tired but at peace. It may help to write down what you are feeling now.

> 4. Think over this and make a mental note of what you have learned. Realise that letting yourself feel sad about something occasionally doesn't make you a negative person. In fact, it is a sign of good mental health to be able to express yourself emotionally. People who try only to have positive feelings are fragile. They need to place restrictions and limits on their experience, because they are unable to handle pressure or conflict well.

You can use this exercise to learn about how you react to any strong emotion and what it means for you. As you learn about the way you respond to different emotions, you will become more emotionally flexible. Allowing yourself to know and feel your emotions allows you to express them – and then let them go. The better you know your emotional self, the better you will be able to care for others.

HOW YOUR EMOTIONS AFFECT YOUR THOUGHTS

As we have already seen, emotions in themselves are neither good nor bad; it's the thoughts our emotions trigger that can sometimes cause problems. For example, sadness is a normal reaction to loss. If someone you love dies it's natural – and desirable – to feel sad. You may think, 'Now xxx has died, I will miss his/her love and company.' The feelings such thoughts lead to are tender, they add to your understanding of yourself and other people, and they add depth to the meaning of life. In this way, it is possible to gain something from your loss. However if, in response to your feelings of sadness, you begin to think, 'Now xxx is dead I'll never be able to be happy again,' your thoughts create feelings of hopelessness, helplessness and lack of energy. The result of such thoughts is depression – a frightening feeling that the world is painted black.

THE FEEL-GOOD FACTOR

Realistically it's not always possible to avoid distressing emotions. However, you can learn to deprive your emotions of their power to sap your energy. This involves looking closely at the things that make you feel bad and then making a conscious decision to change the way you think about them. Fighting against distressing emotions encourages them to flourish and become stronger. Accepting them decreases their power. You always have a choice as to how you deal with your emotions.

Distressing situations don't always go away but you can choose how to react to them. The secret is to find a new way of looking at them, so that they don't seem so important, while at the same time increasing the things that make you feel good about yourself and about life. Use the following six-step plan to help you to reduce stress, to feel more in control of your emotions, and to maintain your zest for life.

> 1. Make a list of all the things that stress, annoy or upset you. Include all the everyday irritations like mislaying your cheque book, or your partner leaving the top off the toothpaste. Ask yourself, 'What upsets me?', 'What makes me feel unhappy?', and 'What makes me feel stressed?' Take your time and think of as many things as you can.
>
> 2. Now go through the things on your list and consider the following questions:
>
> - Can I choose to ignore it? For example, you can choose to ignore your partner leaving the top off the toothpaste and decide that it's his or her problem.
>
> - If you decide you can't ignore it, ask, 'Is there anything I could do about it? What could I do to change what bothers me?' For example, you could ask your partner to put the top on the toothpaste.

- If you don't feel there is anything you can do to change the situation, ask yourself if there is anything you can do to make it go away? For instance, start buying toothpaste in a dispenser?

- If can't avoid it, change it, or make it go away, is there any way I can change my reaction to it? For example, you could decide that there are more things in life to get angry about than leaving the lid off the toothpaste, or reframe the situation so that it seems funny or silly rather than important.

- How can I decide to stop letting it bother me?

- What can I learn from this? What can I find that is good in the thing that bothers me?

3. Now take one or two items from the list and work out a plan of action for making the changes you have decided upon.

4. Now make a list of the things that fill you with fun and vigour. Ask yourself:

- What do I have fun doing?

- What makes me feel enthusiastic?

- Who do I enjoy sharing good experiences with?

- What positive aspects of my life am I taking for granted or ignoring?

5. Now think about how to inject more of the fun things you have identified into your life.

6. Work out a plan of action for increasing the experiences you find revitalising.

You will find that simply doing this exercise enables you to get more of a balance of emotions in your life. You feel more power over your emotions, with the result that you feel less helpless and hopeless and continually learn new ways of making your life better.

Give yourself time. Some pressures you will be able to avoid or get rid of fairly easily. Others may involve a longer time scale. For instance, if you decide your partner's leaving the lid off the toothpaste is just the tip of the iceberg and that your relationship has really had it, it may take some time to sort things out. Some of the fun activities can take longer to put into action. In the long run, however, this is a very practical way to reduce feelings of being unable to cope and replace them with positive anticipation about the future.

Finally, if you really feel you can't do anything to make your life less stressful, perhaps you need to ask yourself what sort of pay-off you are getting from allowing things to stay as they are.

> Ask yourself:
> - What is stopping me from dealing with my situation and finding ways to enjoy my life and work?
> - What benefits am I gaining from leaving things as they are?
> - What payoffs am I getting that make me reluctant to change things?

Were you surprised? Now you are aware of what you are getting from remaining stressed, angry, depressed or whatever, you can decide whether these advantages outweigh the disadvantages, and if they don't, how you are going to deal with your emotions.

FEELING POWER ROUNDUP

You have now learnt how to recognise, accept, express and let go of your emotions. This means that already you are beginning to become stronger and more able to survive the rough times. Check the following list:

> - I am able to recognise the emotions I am feeling
> - I feel confident at expressing my emotions
> - I feel able to control my emotions when necessary
> - I feel confident that I can transform my emotions

In the next chapter you are going to learn about the importance of support when going through bad times and how to get other people on your side. By practising your survival skills in everyday situations, you will be better prepared to face major challenge or change if it occurs.

CHAPTER FOUR
PEOPLE POWER

Other people, our partners, friends, parents, children, and colleagues, are vital to survival. In any situation, but especially when things go wrong, we need to make sense of other people and their actions in order to survive. And we need the help and support of others to help us pull through.

Our first encounter with people was with our parents or those who cared for us when we were young and these relationships set the tone for our later attachments. We are born to love: to ensure that we love and are loved in return we come into this world primed with all the abilities we need to make relationships and ensure that we are cared for. The sucking, clinging, smiling, cooing, crying and babbling of newborn babies are survival mechanisms designed to ensure that those around them love and care for them. And we are programmed to respond: you would have to be hard-hearted indeed to ignore a baby's cry.

If those caring for you make you feel loved and accepted, you come to believe that you are lovable, to find it easy to trust others and to feel secure in your relationships in later life. However, if those caring for you found it hard to love – perhaps because they weren't loved, or were neglected or abused as children – they may have backed off from you as a baby, especially if you were irritable or inattentive (as all babies are from time to time). You may then have learnt that to love and trust others is dangerous and that other people are unreliable. As a result, you may find it hard to become intimate with others in later life.

UNDERSTANDING OTHER PEOPLE

Survivors are those who, whatever their earliest experiences, have learnt to build strong relationships with other people. The ability to be aware of others, to get in touch with their feelings and thoughts and to understand them, is the foundation of people power. This ability is called empathy. To develop it you need to be curious, to allow yourself to receive new information and to be receptive to what your own feelings are telling you about what the other person is thinking and feeling.

Empathy is different from sympathy, which means taking on the same emotions and thoughts someone else has. If a friend loses someone close to them and you cry with them, that is sympathy. When you empathise with someone, you understand and recognise the other person's feelings without having them yourself.

As human beings we each have different ways of experiencing the world. Empathy comes from asking questions like:

- How does this person feel?
- What does this person see?
- What might this person do?
- How does this person experience the world?
- How does this person experience me?

Such questions open your mind and allow you to understand someone else's needs, fears, and views.

To understand the link between empathy and survival, you only have to think about people who are under the domination, control or threat of others. For example, a woman who is in a relationship with a controlling partner has a vested interest in understanding how her partner thinks and behaves. She may spend long hours thinking about him, talking about him and working out how he is going to react and what she can do to please him. The same principle applies to other relationships. For example, in most firms, workers understand the managers better than the managers understand them. People who are disadvantaged, poor or discriminated against are usually street-wise. People who rule, dominate or are in control don't need to live by the same laws and rules they force on others. Their safety and security is assured. They don't need to be tuned into the information that empathy or the wisdom of the streets reveals.

To check your capacity for empathy do this exercise with a friend or colleague you trust:

> 1 Imagine you are your friend or colleague and see how accurately you can describe that person's experience of living or working with you.
>
> 2 Now ask your friend or colleague to tell you how accurate you were.
>
> 3 Reverse roles and see how that person perceives you.

Gaining empathy has the big advantage of allowing you to benefit from other people's experiences. At work, rest or play, the ability to absorb what other people think and feel allows their learning to become your learning so you don't always have to start from scratch.

SPOTTING THE HIDDEN CLUES

Another type of empathy – called pattern empathy – allows you to spot patterns in other people's behaviour and the relationship between cause and effect. This allows you to pick up early clues and predict the likely outcome of certain situations. Top musicians, sportsmen, actors, military leaders and so on, all display the ability to know what to do that comes from having pattern empathy. Tennis players, for example, must learn to read the movements of their opponents so they are able to sense how they will play and what they will do. Such knowledge comes with practice and from taking into account the present game as well as previous games. Conductors of orchestras are able to tune in to dozens of instruments and are able to detect the one player who is playing slowly, softly or off-key and bring them into line with the rest of the orchestra. Playwrights and novelists possess a similar ability to understand the differences between their characters' personality patterns and how they act and react in different circumstances and with each other. This sort of empathy allows you to become aware of all the factors, big and small, that come into play in any situation.

TUNING IN TO THE WAY OTHER PEOPLE EXPERIENCE THE WORLD

Each one of us perceives the world in different ways. As you have already learnt in previous chapters, our experience of the world comes through our bodies, our senses – through sights, sounds, feelings, tastes and smells. Becoming aware of your way of perceiving the world and those of the people around you is one way to develop more empathy. Have a look at the following three main styles of perception. Which one are you?

- **Visual Veronica**. You experience the world through your eyes and what you see. You notice what people look like and what they are wearing. You notice where things take place, the colours of a room or outside scene, whether it is dark or light, bright or dim, or how things are arranged. You are aware of people's movements and gestures and the speed at which things happen. You are likely to pay a lot of attention to the way you dress and to your environment. You may be in a job which reflects this, for example you may be a painter, a designer or be involved in the visual arts. When you write letters you will emphasise the visual aspects of what you are describing and the words you use in conversation will also reflect your style. For example: I see what you mean; I'm looking at the idea; show me what you mean; or my view is coloured by . . .
- **Auditory Aubrey**. You perceive the world mainly through your ears. You will be highly aware of the accent and rhythm of people's speech. You will be highly sensitive to noise, and aware of how far away noise is coming from and where it is. You probably love listening to music and going

to concerts and have a large CD collection. Your job or hobby may involve using your voice or playing music. You prefer talking on the phone to writing letters and when you are describing an event or situation your conversation will be peppered with sound language such as: we're on the same wavelength; I intend to turn a deaf ear to the situation; or that rings a bell.

- **Kinaesthetic Kathy**. Kinaesthesia is the sense of touch and bodily sensations. It can also include taste and smell. If you are kinaesthetic, you perceive the world through what you feel, smell and taste. You are highly aware of the weight and texture of things and people, whether they are soft or hard, rough or smooth. You love food and cooking, the texture and flavour of food and its aroma. Your job may draw on these bodily sensations: weaver, tailor or textile worker, aromatherapist, chef or cook. In your spare time you may go swimming and be highly aware of the feel of the water on your skin, or like eating out. You are less interested in the colours of the clothes you wear than their textures and you love perfumes and scent your rooms with aromatherapy oils or joss sticks. Your language reflects all this and you use expressions such as: I'll be in touch; I can't grasp what you are saying; I can't quite put my finger on it; or she's a smooth operator.

You can tune into those around you and build a rapport by being aware of their style of perception. You will then be able to communicate with them in terms they will understand. For example, if your partner is a Visual Veronica and you are telling her about a football match, she will be far more interested if you describe it in terms of visual images: the colours the players were wearing, the speed with which they moved, the position of the players at different times on the field and so on.

'I HAD NO IDEA IT WAS GOING TO HAPPEN'

Many of us say that we had no idea that a crisis in a relationship was going to happen. However, sometimes we did know, but chose to ignore the clues. You have already learnt about the importance of listening to your body. Another vital survival skill is the ability to 'read' other people's non-verbal language and become aware of the unspoken messages that lie behind what is being said out loud. Listen carefully, with all your senses and you will discover that the words people use sometimes contradict the way they are saying them. It can be something small that alerts you: a tone of voice, something not said, a sudden silence, a forced laugh, someone's quick glance – anything that doesn't fit. Once you are aware of this, even if it is only a vague feeling, relax and try to focus on what is happening.

Developing this sort of empathy allows you to tap into 'hidden agendas' and spot the real messages that may be concealed behind what other people are saying. You develop the ability to hear with all your senses and not just take events and people at face value. To see how good you are at spotting hidden clues try the following exercise:

> 1. Think back to a relationship you had that turned out badly. It could be a love affair, a business partnership, friendship or other relationship that didn't work out as you wanted.
>
> 2. Now list as many early signs or warnings that you had that things were going wrong. Think about what the other person said, how s/he behaved, his or her body language and so on.

Chances are that, as you will remember when we looked at the five steps of change in Chapter One, there were clues that things weren't going well, but you chose to ignore them. If you follow the steps we talked about in learning from experience in that chapter you will be able to decide how to play things so they turn out better next time.

DEALING WITH DIFFICULT PEOPLE

Learning how to deal with difficult people is an important skill in the survivor personality. It helps to remember that people aren't 'difficult' in themselves; it is their behaviour that is difficult. Understanding the roots of people's difficult behaviour – in other words, developing empathy with them – can help you get on with them better.

Most of us attribute difficult behaviour to sheer stubbornness, but sometimes such behaviour can be a result of fear or anxiety, a conflict of values or needs (what we consider is important), or a difference in personality or style (see above). Learning to distinguish the attitudes and ways of behaving from the person expressing them enables you to cope without judging.

Difficult people come in many forms:

- **The moaners.** Moaners are always complaining. Nothing ever goes their way, and when it does they are never satisfied. They criticise your suggestions and your plans, so that when things go wrong it's never their fault. Whatever happens – even if it is something good – they find something bad to say. Deep down, they fear failure. And the way to avoid failure is not to try in the first place.
- **The bully.** Bullies are loud, aggressive, tense and tyrannical. Whenever you do anything they judge, blame and disagree. Bullies see themselves as above everyone else. When something goes wrong they love to say, 'I told you so' or 'It's not my fault, I tried to warn you.' Whatever happens, bullies have to be the boss, because deep down they feel lonely and unimportant.
- **The pacifier.** Pacifiers never like to disagree with anyone. They agree with everything you have to say and defend other people's actions – but always very gently. They see themselves as peacemakers, but come across as ingratiating and helpless. Deep down, they feel worthless; this results in a need to please, making them afraid to express their own

opinions. When things go wrong, they are able to deny responsibility.
- **The robot.** Robots like to see everything logically. They believe that they act completely rationally and objectively. At all times, they try to give the impression of being calm and collected, but often come across as unfeeling, cut-off and distant. Deep down, robots feel vulnerable and threatened by closeness and the open expression of emotions, while at the same time longing for them. Their ability to argue away others' attempts to change their attitudes allows them to believe they don't need them.
- **The butterfly.** You never know where you are with a butterfly, because s/he never stays on one subject for more than a moment. They make irrelevant statements, fail to respond to the points you make, try to do half a dozen things at once, and flit from plan to plan. They appear dizzy, childish and ungrounded. As a result you feel unsettled and confused. Other people rarely turn to a butterfly for advice and support. However, deep down, butterflies have a chronic need for attention and caring. Their lives lack direction because they don't feel they belong anywhere.
- **The avoider.** Avoiders come across as aloof and superior. They never engage with you, pretend not to understand, make excuses, or pretend to be absent-minded or forgetful. They come across as weak and reticent. By avoiding other people, they ensure that people don't bother them. Avoiders are rarely asked to join groups or go to parties. In fact, deep down, avoiders are afraid of the world and of being rejected. Their deepest need is for someone to care for them.

Of course, these are all stereotypes, but if you think about them you will almost certainly be able to recognise aspects of your own behaviour and those of people you know.

> Try another exercise in empathy:
>
> 1. Think about the stereotypes above and whether any of them seem familiar. If they do, try to flesh them out by adding aspects of your own behaviour.
>
> 2. Now think about any difficult people in your life and try to identify what it is in the way they behave that you find difficult. Don't censor their behaviour, simply describe it.
>
> 3. Now try to imagine what it is like to be that person and think about why they might behave in the way they do, using the insights you have gained in this chapter. Think about the pay-offs they may gain from being the way they are. These could include:
>
> - Gaining attention.
> - Avoiding failure
> - Being prepared for the worst
> - Being able to say, 'I told you so'
> - Not being burdened by other people's problems
> - Avoiding responsibility for things that go wrong
> - Avoiding difficulties
>
> Can you think of any others?

By doing this exercise, you have already started to develop empathy with the difficult people in your life. This will enable you to react to them in a more creative and relaxed way. Bear in mind these three points:

- Your distress, frustration and lack of success with this person are signs that you don't understand them
- Stop blaming them for their behaviour. Remember that you can't change other people, but you can change yourself and

your reactions. This immediately takes off some of the
pressure.
- Try to think about what makes that person behave in the
  way s/he does. Be curious. What are they gaining from
  being 'difficult'. Why do they repeat their negative patterns
  over and over again?

Feeling better? You should be. You have now learned that the way you deal with negative people is to change the way you think about them and that this puts you in control. No longer are you at the mercy of those around you, you are in charge of your emotions and reactions. In fact, the difficulty is an opportunity to learn more about yourself and other people and to develop more flexible ways of handling what other people do. And, of course, flexibility is of the essence in the survivor personality.

WAYS TO HANDLE DIFFICULT PEOPLE

Now let's look at some specific ways of dealing with difficult people. Bear in mind that there is no right or wrong way. The point is to be flexible:

- **Be honest.** Acknowledge and accept what the difficult person is saying and then let them know how it is affecting you. Try saying, 'What you are telling me isn't helping us to solve the problem, and it upsets me to hear you saying all these negative things.'
- **Agree with them.** Often the best way to deal with something is not to oppose it, but to respond in kind and go with it. By not arguing back, you present difficult people with a problem. And often they change their mind. Try saying, 'You know, after listening to you carefully, I think you are right,' – and then change the subject. When you do this difficult people are often so surprised that they start to argue back against their own arguments and you can begin to make progress.
- **Be firm.** If you declare your limits you may be surprised at how sensitive and considerate the difficult person becomes.

Try saying, 'I can't deal with the way you are behaving/what you are saying at the moment. Please stop.'

- **Be rude.** Many of us have been brought up to believe that it is not polite to ignore people. However, since attention is a big pay-off for many difficult people, ignoring their negative statements or behaviour by not paying attention to them is one way to stop them. It takes guts to be rude and go against the grain of your good manners, but it might just work. Another rude (yet often effective) tactic is to tell them to shut up. Try saying, 'Your moaning bothers me. I don't need it right now. Please don't talk to me like that.'
- **Tell them they are wrong.** It can sometimes help to say matter of factly, 'You're wrong. It's a shame you think like that'. Don't attempt to explain, just state it as a fact. Then wait to see if they ask. You may still get into an argument but you often stand more chance of being heard if you state your own opinion categorically first.
- **Tell them they are right.** Playing difficult people at their own game can be highly effective. Listen to what they are saying for a while and then respond in kind. Try saying, 'The situation is much worse than you imagine,' and then proceed to describe all the things there are to be upset about. Most people respond by saying, 'It's not that bad' and you have turned their complaints on their head.
- **Be sympathetic.** Just as children cry when they are upset to gain attention and express their feelings, adults may complain. It's not acceptable for adults to cry. What they can get away with is expressing their unhappiness. Sometimes moaning is a form of crying.
- **Accept and acknowledge their behaviour.** Sometimes people who are negative want it to be known that they are predicting failure. In this way, if things fall through, they are not to blame but they can take some of the credit if things go well. By accepting and acknowledging their dire predictions you lessen their anxiety. Don't try to change negative talk if it's working in your favour.

- **Make the difficult person an ally.** It's human nature to identify with others. This means that in groups poor decisions are sometimes made because disagreements are suppressed. Difficult people can be useful in helping to identify and solve problems. Ask them to be negative about a plan to help you to define the difficulties. Tell them that describing the problem is a first step to solving it. Praise them for being experts at predicting what will not work out. Now ask them for help in solving the problem they have identified. Make them describe the goal. Then ask them to develop an action plan for solving it.

Feeling more confident? You should be. The list above is a tool kit for dealing with difficult people. It shows that there is not just one way to react to pessimism, negativity or moaning. You don't have to be a victim. You do have a choice. Remember what counts is to discover the way that works best for you with that person.

It is important to remember that if someone who is normally pleasant to be around becomes difficult, there is usually a reason for it and they need your help. The suggestions above are for people who are always negative or difficult.

HOW TO HANDLE ANGRY PEOPLE

Dealing with other people's anger is a vital skill for survivors. As with dealing with difficult people, you have several choices. However, anger is such a strong emotion that it is often difficult to decide how to react when faced with someone who is angry. Before we look at effective ways of dealing with other people's anger, check the following list and tick any tactics you use.

When dealing with someone who is angry I:

- Get angry back
- Refuse to listen
- Tell them to stop being angry
- Make fun of them or criticise them
- Deny what they are saying

- Dismiss what they are saying as unimportant
- Say, 'Yes, but . . .' (another way of denying the validity of what they are saying)

Recognise any of them? If you do, you will probably be aware that they don't work. In fact, behaving in these ways is almost certain not just to maintain the conflict, but even to escalate it.

The good news is that you can learn to deal with angry people more effectively. Remember that often when people are angry, their anger is not aimed at you directly. You just happen to be the person in the firing line. So try not to take it personally. Take a deep breath, relax and stay centred. Even if the anger is directly aimed at you, try to stay calm. The following five-step plan is a tried and tested way of dealing with other people's anger.

- **Step one: Ask what is wrong.** People can't hear when they are talking, still less when they are ranting and raving, so the first step is to interrupt what they are saying and pull their anger towards you. By asking what is wrong you are conveying to the angry person that you are really interested in what has upset them, and that you expect to be able to handle it. At this stage don't try to explain your side of the matter. People who are angry and upset need to discharge their emotions before being capable of listening to reason. If you can, get the person to sit down – it's harder to stay angry and upset when you are sitting down. Try to convey your empathy by sitting close to them and leaning slightly forwards.
- **Step two: Listen.** As the angry person tells you what is wrong listen carefully to what s/he has to say. Convey that you are listening by nodding your head, looking at the person attentively and encouraging them to continue. You don't have to agree with them, but do show you have heard and acknowledge what they are saying by expressions such as 'Uh-huh'. Ask clarifying questions, such as when, where, why or who. Repeat back things the person has said. This stops the flow of anger and helps the person to calm down.

It may even help to write down the points, both to help you remember and to show the person you are listening.

- **Step three: Stay with the angry person.** Even if you disagree with what the person is saying, you can acknowledge what they are feeling. You might say something like, 'It's understandable that you feel upset. Let's have a look at what we can do about it.' Try to make a difference between agreeing with what the person is saying and acknowledging what they are feeling. For example, saying, 'You shouldn't feel upset' is alienating and can make the angry person feel even more upset.
- **Step four: Find areas of agreement.** Tell the person if there are any aspects of the thing that is making them angry that you do agree with and ask them what solution they suggest. Thank them for pointing out what is upsetting them. After all, you may find that you learn information that proves useful in solving the problem. An even more advanced skill is to add more arguments in favour of the person's anger. This shows the person that you understand what they are going through and why they are feeling angry. For example, 'And besides that you've got a lot else on your mind. You can do without this.'
- **Step five: Describe the problem or goal.** Now you have understood the problem and found some areas of agreement, you are ready to resolve the problem. Describe to the angry person the problem or goal that lies behind their anger and ask for suggestions as to how to handle it. Once they have begun to calm down, as they probably will have if you have followed the above steps, you can say, 'This is the problem we have if we don't do X. Can you suggest a better solution?' Don't assume that you know what the angry person wants to achieve; let them tell you. Or better still, ask them.

The five-step plan isn't infallible, of course, but it gives you a better chance than the strategies described earlier, and you will often find that people respond more positively than you imagine.

PEOPLE YOU CAN LEAN ON

As well as developing empathy and learning how to deal with other people, you need to know how to get the support you need when things go wrong. Study after study of survivors has shown that an important factor has been the support of others. Support means being able to share your emotions and feelings with others when things go wrong. The person who offers you support may be your partner, friend, colleague, relative or member of a self-help group – or a combination of any of these.

Not all supportive relationships are healthy. For example, some of your supporters may have a vested interest in keeping you dependent on them, and not encouraging you to solve your problems for yourself, because it boosts their self-esteem and makes them feel stronger and more powerful. To determine the quality of the support you can call on in times of trouble, have a think about your support network. Make a list of the people you can call on. Now go through the list and answer the following questions:

> 1. What sort of support does this person give you? Make a list of their qualities.
>
> 2. Who do they remind you of? For example, your mother, a teacher, a friend?
>
> 3. What would happen if this person was no longer able to support you? What would you lose and what would you gain?
>
> 4. In what ways do you find the relationship with this person supportive and in what ways is it not supportive?

The experts have identified three different types of support:

- Nurturing support which helps prepare you to solve your problems

- Energizing support which helps you develop creative solutions to your problems
- Relaxing support which helps you to recharge your energies

Think about what sort of support you gain from each of the people you lean on. You may find that you are getting too much of one type of support and too little of another. It can help to discuss this with the people you call on for support.

Support isn't just a one-way ticket. Supportive relationships need nourishment and maintenance, just like other types of relationship. Looking at the relationship you have with the people you call on for support can help you to become a better supporter yourself, when they hit bad times. Once the crisis or challenge that you are facing has passed it can help to sit down with your supporter, perhaps over a cup of tea or a glass of wine, and take turns to ask the following:

- Who are you for me?
- What do you contribute to our relationship and what do I contribute to it?

Discuss your answers and whether you both feel happy with the relationship as it is and the amount you each contribute. Now ask the other person to do three specific things for you, which you know they can do, and ask him or her to make three requests of you.

All relationships have rules and supportive ones are no exception. The following questions can help you draw up a contract with the person you are hoping will support you. This ensures that both of you know where you are and helps avoid misunderstandings and resentments. You can apply them to finding a professional supporter such as a counsellor or therapist or to enlisting the help of a friend, relative or colleague if you are in trouble:

- What am I looking for in the way of support?
- Who among my friends, relatives or colleagues can I ask to give me this support? Do I need to seek professional help?
- Ask the other person what they want and how the relationship will meet their needs? Is it money (professional therapist)? Friendship? Reciprocal support? Involvement

in a self-help group? Having their dinner cooked? Regular phone calls or letters?
- Work out what your commitment to the relationship will be. What sort of time commitment do you require? Talking to your supporter on the phone whenever you feel blue? Arranging to meet once a month in a wine bar? Going to a regular meeting or support group? Attending a regular therapy session once a week?

Think about when, how often and where you will meet and what sort of relationship you will have. In the case of professional support, any payment should be clearly outlined and agreed.

PEOPLE POWER ROUNDUP

Now you have learnt how to create satisfying relationships complete the following checklist:

- I feel confident in my ability to form strong relationships with a number of different people
- I feel able to empathise with the people I meet and understand why they feel and act as they do even if I don't agree with them
- I feel confident that I can deal with difficult people in an assertive way without being manipulated or bullied
- I feel able to identify the sort of support I need in various situations and the people who can give me that support

Right. Now you have developed some people skills, you are ready to find out how to tap into the power of your mind so as to enhance your ability to survive.

CHAPTER FIVE
MIND POWER

Your mind and the way you think are vital to your ability to survive. Many non-survivors go under when they encounter difficult situations simply as a result of the way they think. Before we start to look at how you can develop your thinking power, let's quell three common myths that can crop up when people start thinking about survival.

Check the following statements and say whether you consider them true or false:

- 'To become a survivor I'll have to make big changes in the way I think'

False. Just by living your life until now you have already developed some survival strategies, though most of the time you may be unaware of them. Being a survivor doesn't mean having to make major reconstructions in the way you think. However, you will learn how to be more conscious of who you are and what is going on inside your mind. Sometimes you will have to make small but important adjustments in the way you think.

- 'To become a survivor I'll have to spend a lot of time combating my present negative thoughts'

False. You have already found some advice on handling negative or unhelpful thoughts and you will discover some more in this chapter. However the main focus is on developing survivor ways of thinking.

Most of the time you will find the new ways of thinking are so successful that they automatically replace your old patterns of thought without you even thinking about it.

- 'Now I have started to think and behave like a survivor, nothing bad will ever happen to me again'

False. Unfortunately, developing a survivor personality won't stop bad things from happening. It can, however, stop you from behaving in such a way that you bring misfortune on yourself. And it can also protect you from being being completely devastated by the bad things that happen. Don't expect miracles, and try not to be discouraged if it takes a little time. You will find some of the insights and exercises here useful; others may not work so well. Carry on reading, keep the ones that work for you and discard the others.

DEVELOPING YOUR THINKING POWER

Studies of survivors have shown that intelligence – the ability to use the mind – is an important asset. Intelligence is more than how 'clever' you believe you are or how well you did at school. Rather, it is about learning to use your mental capacities to the full, so you can decide how to react to the challenges that come your way and solve problems creatively.

Our brains have two sides. Your left brain is concerned with cause and effect, thinking logically, analytically and in straight lines. Your right brain works by flashes of inspiration, making connections, imagination, emotional response, fantasy, dream and intuition. Both parts of the brain are important, as US brain researcher Marilyn Ferguson has observed: 'Cut off from the fantasy, dreams, intuitions of the right brain, the left is sterile. And the right brain, cut off from integration with its organising partner, keeps recycling its emotional charge . . .' Part of the survivor's flexibility is the ability to call on both sides of the brain to solve problems.

CHILDHOOD LESSONS

You started to think the way you do even before you were born. As babies, we play an active part in our own mental development: learning about the world and the way things work by observation, investigation and experiment. As we grow and develop, we become more mentally agile. At six months, a shoe may be something to put in your mouth to gnaw on, at three years it may represent a telephone which you put to your ear and talk into, at five you may mentally compute the number of eyelets it has.

Each one of us acquires our own unique thinking style, which helps us to decide on the way to approach problems and process information. Some of us as children respond to problems quickly and intuitively, others take their time to assess the various paths open to them before arriving at an answer. Some of us are 'divergent' or creative thinkers, able to generate lots of alternative ideas or solutions to problems, others are 'convergent' thinkers, using analysis or logic to pick out the one best answer to a problem. If your parents encouraged you to be independent, curious and playful and allowed you the freedom to explore new possibilities you are likely to develop your creative side more. Intriguingly, from a survivor point of view, it's also been discovered that a surprising number of leading artists, musicians and other creative people experienced lonely, insecure and unhappy childhoods. Creativity then is an important survival skill – not surprising when you consider that basically it is a flexible, self-reliant response.

Our mental abilities are amazingly varied. You may have a talent for language, a way with words; you may be musical and have an acute sensitivity to sound patterns; you may be logical and mathematical; you may, like an artist or sculptor, be very spatially aware, with an ability to perceive and transform what you see; you may have, like dancers and athletes, the ability to perform 'intelligent' movement; or you may have a strong personal and social awareness, an exceptional sensitivity to your own inner life and that of other people.

Whatever your mental skills and talents, your beliefs about them can affect how successfully you meet challenges. If you were told that you weren't clever or if you didn't do well academically, you may lack self-confidence in your mental abilities and skills. Self-confidence and the belief that you can bring your mental skills to bear on the problems that life throws at you are vital to survival. Bear in mind that labels such as 'not clever' often reflect the fact that your thinking style was different from the rest of your family or the logical, linguistic and mathematical thinking style valued at school.

TAPPING IN TO YOUR MENTAL SKILLS

All of us take for granted mental abilities and thinking skills that come into play in the things that we do. Wherever your talents lie – whether it's in planning parties, talking to people, working out who did it in a murder mystery, dancing flamenco, driving, or speaking foreign languages – your thinking skills are unique to you. What's more, you can learn to tap into them to increase your ability to survive. The first step is to become aware of what they are. For example, dancing flamenco involves a bodily-kinaesthetic awareness that includes using your right brain to respond to your partner and imagining how to express the music. It also includes using your left brain to plan routines and moves and co-ordinate your movements. Speaking languages involves a way with words. You use your left brain to work out the structure of the language and its grammar, and your right brain to create your own words and phrases, respond to others and pick up nuances of meaning. To tune into your thinking style, try the following exercise. You will need a pen and notebook.

> 1. Think of some things you are good at and enjoy doing and write them down.
>
> 2. Now think about each of these things and the mental skills and talents you use to do them. These might be logical steps you perform, or it could include an image or a comparison, like 'making a mental map' or 'sorting through my mental filing cabinet'.

> 3. Now compare the various activities you have listed and see which of them involve the same mental activities and which you apply different skills to.

Doing this exercise enables you to identify the mental skills you apply to things that you do and so to become aware of your unique thinking style. To develop that style, you now need to start applying your particular style to life's challenges. For example, if you discovered that your hobby of playing tennis involved visualising the moves your opponent was going to make, you can consciously choose to apply the same mental skill next time you have an argument with your boss. If logical, step-by-step thinking is your forte, apply that to solving problems. If you rely on gathering lots of information, then letting it stew in your mind for a day or so before getting a 'sudden' flash of inspiration, apply the same process to other tasks.

As you experiment with your different ways of thinking, you will become more mentally agile and creative in dealing life's challenges.

HOW TO THRIVE IN THE FACE OF CHANGE

Who is responsible for the way your life goes? Your answer to this question reveals one of the most important beliefs in the survivor personality. One of the key qualities survivors share is the belief that they are in charge of their own destiny. If, on the other hand, you believe that outside forces and other people are responsible for the way your life goes, you are more likely to feel numb, victimised, helpless or angry in the face of change. The following exercise will uncover your beliefs.

> Tick the statements that reflect what you think best:
>
> 1. a) Success at work comes from being in the right place at the right time/knowing the right people

> b) Success at work comes from hard work and persistence
>
> 2. a) My income is more a matter of luck than ability
>
>   b) My income is determined mostly by my ability
>
> 3. a) I have little control over the things that happen to me
>
>   b) I usually deserve the things that happen to me
>
> 4. a) Success or failure depends largely on luck
>
>   b) Success largely depends on good planning and hard work
>
> 5. a) I would be happier if it weren't for wars, famine, disease and all the other problems in the world
>
>   b) I can be happy even though there are so many problems in the world

How to score: if you ticked mainly 'a's, you believe that what happens is out of your control and you are likely to find it harder to thrive in difficult situations. If you ticked mainly 'b's, you believe you are in charge of your own life and what happens to you. This makes it easier for you to survive – and thrive – when things go wrong.

Intriguingly whatever you believe tends to prove itself. So, if you believe your fate is in the stars, then you will act in a way that confirms your beliefs. If you believe you can do things to make your life better, your actions will confirm this. Learning to believe in yourself can help you survive both the big changes that happen to you and the small, constant ones.

LEARNING TO THINK WELL OF YOURSELF

In all the studies that have been done of survivors, high self-esteem – the ability to think well of yourself – comes high on the list of survival qualities. Having a healthy sense of your own worth enables you to believe in yourself and your ability to deal with problems. If you have high self-esteem, your good opinion of yourself acts like a thick security blanket. It allows you to shrug off hurtful criticism, to appreciate compliments, and to have a realistic idea of your strengths and weaknesses. High self-esteem leads to self-confidence, your belief in yourself and your expectations of how well you will cope in any situation. If you lack self-confidence, you may feel that you cannot rely on yourself and so avoid taking risks. As a result, you suffer great anxiety if you have to deal with new or unfamiliar situations and approach problems beset with doubts and fear of failure.

To see how well you think of yourself try the following exercise.

Tick the statements that apply to you:

- I frequently doubt my ability to get what I want
- I have a strong need to control others
- I often belittle my own achievements
- I often feel that I have to prove myself
- I prefer doing what I am told rather than being responsible for my own actions
- I fear taking risks because they might not turn out well
- I frequently set limits on what I believe I can do
- I get nervous when people compliment me or I deflect the compliment
- When faced with a challenge I often fear I won't be able to meet it

> • I often have problems with power and control in my relationships

How did you get on? The more boxes you ticked, the lower your self-esteem, but don't despair. Remember that the ability to survive is built by exposing yourself to challenge. Try to learn to see life's challenges, changes and crises as opportunities to build up your inner worth, and gain the self-confidence you need to deal with new situations. Check out the following benefits of high self-esteem and self-confidence and then decide that you are going to take steps to boost your inner sense of worth.

> Having strong self-esteem and self-confidence will allow you to:
>
> - recover from major set backs like unemployment, divorce, disfigurement or the loss of someone you love
> - set challenging goals for yourself and handle your success when it occurs
> - accept and feel you deserve praise, recognition and friendship
> - do the things you want to do, and not those you feel pressured into out of fear of displeasing other people
> - resist being manipulated by insincere flattery
> - reject undeserved criticism
> - admit your mistakes and apologise for them
> - handle new, unexpected developments in the knowledge that you can count on yourself
> - build your identity as a unique and special human being

GETTING YOURSELF ON YOUR SIDE

The key to developing a strong sense of self-esteem is to separate the way you feel and think about yourself from the way others feel about you. At first, you may find this difficult to do, but once you start practising it becomes easier. To help you get started try the following exercise. You will need a pen and notebook.

Take two pages of your notebook and make two lists:

1. Things I like about myself
   ....
   ....
   ....
   ....

2. Things I am good at doing
   ....
   ....
   ....
   ....

For the first list, spend some time thinking about all your good points: your physical appearance, your social skills, events, experiences, thoughts and feelings that you feel particularly pleased about or proud of, or risks taken. For the second list, think of your skills and abilities: things you have achieved or done well, big or small, how you can stand up for your beliefs and appreciating your surroundings.

Now look at your two lists and allow yourself to bathe in the glow of your positive comments.

Doing these exercises helps you to buffer yourself against insensitive comments from others, so that you can deflect criticism, strengthen yourself and sustain yourself psychologically. They also allow you to recognise your strengths and help you gain confidence that you can cope with whatever happens because you have strengths that you can bring to bear, and because you have coped in the past.

BARRIERS TO SURVIVAL

Defence mechanisms are ways of behaving that we use to protect ourselves in the face of stress or change. The higher your self-esteem, the fewer defence mechanisms you will need because you will have the inner certainty that you can deal with challenge. This is important because often the defences we use are harmful to ourselves or others and can stop us from dealing with problems effectively.

> Tick any of the following list of defence mechanisms that apply to you.
>
> Faced with a difficult or painful situation or relationship:
>
> - I go blank, withdraw or blush
> - I don't know what to say so I don't say anything
> - I tell myself it doesn't matter
> - I go onto the attack before I can be hurt
> - I refuse to move from the position I've taken – even if it becomes untenable
> - I tell myself I'm bored even though I know it's not true
> - I put myself down by telling myself I must be stupid
> - I override anyone who disagrees with me
> - I retreat behind a newspaper/read a novel/switch on the TV/play with my computer
> - I play the clown to distract myself and others from the true problem
> - I laugh nervously
> - I change the subject and pretend I haven't heard what was said

> Add any other defence mechanisms that you habitually use...
>
> ....

Defence mechanisms often come into play when a situation we find ourselves in conjures up an occasion when we felt we couldn't cope in the past. It can be something someone says. Sometimes it's not the words themselves that you hear but how they say it – the loudness, tone of voice or the speed. These can spark off a memory a particular scene, a sudden feeling that you've been here before.

Learn to recognise that defence mechanisms may have served a useful purpose in the past, but that now they are limiting you rather than enabling you to survive. If you find yourself acting in a defensive way try the following exercise:

> 1. Sit down, relax, close your eyes, and let the feelings you are experiencing about a particular person or situation wash over you. Think about the situation and conjure it up in as much detail as you possibly can. Is the room hot or cold? Is it dark or light? What sights and sounds can you hear?
>
> 2. Once you have conjured up the situation or person and the feelings, mentally let go of this situation, hold onto the feeling, and let yourself slide down a mental time tunnel into your childhood. When can you remember feeling those feelings before? Don't force it. If you hold onto the feelings for long enough, something will come.
>
> 3. Now ask yourself the following questions:
>
> - What am I defending myself against?
> - Why do I need to defend myself?
> - Do I need to change my defence mechanisms?

Do this every time you find yourself reacting defensively and you will learn to let these mechanisms go and behave in a more flexible way.

- *A case of mistaken jealousy*
  Tricia saw her partner talking to a pretty woman and felt a sudden spurt of jealousy, rage and fear. She flounced out of the party in tears and when they got home immediately accused her partner of intending to be unfaithful – somewhat of an over-reaction! On taking time to track the scenario back, Tricia discovered that the first time she experienced those feelings was when, as a child of three, her parents sent her away to stay with her aunt. When she returned, she discovered she had a baby sister. The underlying fear of abandonment kicked into action when she saw her partner flirting because it triggered an unconscious memory of the first time she had felt those feelings. Once she realised this, she was able to respond more calmly to her partner's flirtation and even enjoy flirting a little herself, safe in the knowledge that she loved and was loved in return.

BEAT YOUR MENTAL SABOTEURS

We're now going to look at some of the mental barriers, or saboteurs, that can get in the way of developing survival skills and look at ways to beat them.

BEAT! 'Oh, no! This can't be happening to me'. It can – and it is. Don't allow yourself to wallow in self-pity and bear in mind that you are not alone. Send yourself some supportive messages. For example, 'This has happened to other people besides me and they have survived.' Or 'I'm not the only person ever to run into this problem.'

ACTION! You may like to talk to other people who have gone through the same experience that you are now going through, perhaps among your friends, relatives or colleagues or by contacting a support group. Let them talk about their experiences and ask what they learned from it and what was valuable for them. How did they cope? Did they talk to themselves – if so, what sort of things did they say? Did they hold particular goals in mind? Try not to make assumptions about what their answers will be and be prepared to make unexpected findings.

BEAT! 'Disaster struck me out of the blue'. Learn to recognise that most troubles don't just happen. True, there are some occasions when no one could have anticipated something happening. This is a crisis. However, there is often a pattern to 'unexpected' problems. And, as we've already seen, becoming aware of the path you are travelling on allows you to foresee obstacles or difficulties so you can plan to survive them.

ACTION! Try to track back through all the possible causes of the disaster you are now facing. Then go through your list and pinpoint the three most likely causes. These can often point the way to possible solutions. Make sure you check any solutions you come up with to make sure they address the causes you have identified. If you get into the habit of doing this, you will find it easier to solve problems.

BEAT! 'I'll never be able to survive'. You can and you will. Think of situations you have encountered in the past where you have overcome obstacles and found the courage to cope. These may be of two types: similar situations in the past where you were able to marshall your survival skills to cope, and other difficult situations that you got through.

ACTION! Make a list of survival skills that you harnessed in the past, and recall how you dealt with previous problems. Concentrate on the positive factors in your survival, rather than dwelling on the negative ones.

BEAT! 'It's not funny'. Well, it could be, if you changed your way of thinking about it. There are few situations that are so black that it is not possible to see the funny side of them – even if it is 'graveyard humour'. Learning to see the funny side of things can help buffer you against life's bumps and knocks and make the situation more tolerable.

ACTION! Find out what makes you laugh and then apply it to the situation you are now facing. Build up a collection of funny books, videos, stories and so on that you can turn to when life is getting you down. Arrange to spend time with a friend who makes you laugh.

BEAT! 'There is no alternative'. There always is an alternative so long as you are prepared to think creatively about your problems. Finding the alternative involves acknowledging that you are blocked, scrapping your original plan and redrawing it.

ACTION! Distance yourself from your original goals by looking at them and analysing why they are not working. Changing the way you think often helps, so try to think of other ways of viewing the problem. List all the possible new solutions you can think of to get across the barrier. Don't censor them, however ridiculous they appear. Now look at these and think about which ones might work. Give yourself time and don't make hasty decisions. If you don't try to force it, your brain will often do the work for you.

MIND POWER ROUNDUP

You have now become aware of your mind and your own personal thinking style. You know that if you learn to trust your own thought processes, they can help you survive. Take some time to think about your present state of mind. Consider how you can develop your individual thinking style and powers. Now check the following list:

- I enjoy my mind and the way I think
- I am aware of how the way I think influences my self-esteem and self-confidence
- I intend to listen to my mind and what it is telling me
- I feel mentally competent and resilient

> - I feel able to beat the mental barriers I have erected that are holding me back

OK? Now you are ready to find out about the importance of time and the part that it plays in your survival.

CHAPTER SIX
GOOD TIMES, BAD TIMES

Time is very important to the survivor. All of us live in time. And as time passes things change. The pace of change has gone into overdrive in the past few decades. For our parents and grandparents, change was usually a one-off upheaval to be gone through before life settled back to its normal routine. Today we live lives of constant change. Your father and grandfather probably left school or university and went into a job for life; today, most of us expect to change our work several times. In the past, too, it was unusual for a company to change hands more than once in a worker's lifetime, divorce was a rare occurence, a notice from your building society telling you it has been taken over was a rare event; today, all these things happen every day.

TIME CHANGES THINGS

In order to deal with change, you first need to be aware that it is happening. Have a look at a time of depression and uncertainty from your own experience in which the present is different from the past.

PAST	PRESENT
• Marriage	• Living together
• Staying with one partner for life	• Having several partners
• Being 'on the shelf'	• Choosing to stay single
• Two-parent families	• One-parent families
• Having large families	• Having small families
• Families living nearby	• Families spread across the country/world
• Children watched by older adults	• Children watch TV
• Children invent own games	• Bought toys and computer games
• Right ways to behave	• Choices of behaviour
• One religion	• Different religions
• Men the main breadwinners	• Women going out to work
• Clearcut rules for men and women	• 'New man' and liberated woman
• Corner shops	• Out-of-town supermarkets
• Books	• The Internet
• Records	• CDs
• Doctor knows best	• Patient power
• Orthodox medicine	• Alternative medicine
• Future certain	• Future uncertain

• Reliance on leaders	• Reliance on self
• One job for life	• Many changes of work and job
• Eliminate stress	• Handle stress
• Avoid mistakes	• Learn from mistakes
• Die earlier	• Live longer

The secret of surviving change is to commit yourself to carrying on learning throughout life. To do this you need to be able to let go of the past. The 'good old days' will never return – and chances are they weren't always as good as you remember them. One way of dealing emotionally with letting go of the past is to get together with others and talk about your memories. What are you proud of? What do you feel sad to lose? What are you glad to have got away from? Now think about what is better now than before. What is good about all the changes that are taking place?

THE TIME OF YOUR LIFE

As well as the changes taking place in the world around us, our lives are in a process of constant change. Psychologists often talk about 'life tasks', challenges we face and goals we want to achieve, which appear on our life agenda at particular times. Your life tasks represent your hopes and dreams and reflect your personal history and the way you see the world. They are the things that you consider important: areas of excitement, opportunity . . . and vulnerability.

Certain life tasks typically crop up at particular periods of our lives. For example, in the late teens and early twenties most of us are facing the life task of learning to live on our own, away from our families. Throughout our lives we encounter turning points when we move from one life stage to another. At these times of transition, our life tasks often become clearer and we develop new goals in the hope of creating positive change in our lives and personalities. At such points, we may become acutely aware of ourselves and our place in the world as we face new life tasks. You can use these turning points as opportunities to increase your skills for survival and develop your resilience.

ESCAPING 'THE CHEMISTRY OF THE MOMENT'

Becoming aware of the types of tasks that are likely to crop up over the course of your lifetime and having some idea of the time scale involved allows you to prepare and plan ahead, so you are able to deal with them in the most effective way. Psychiatrist Michael Rutter, who has made the study of resilience his life work, believes that one of the most vital keys to survival is to escape what he calls the 'chemistry of the moment'. The ability to survive comes not just from what happens at the time of a difficult or painful experience, but also from what has happened before and what happens after it.

To survive, we need to take a long view, to see how events from our past can have repercussions in the present, and how these can affect our future. We need to learn how to overcome the results of things that have happened to us in the past and find ways of arming ourselves against adversity in the future. As the writer Daniel Levinson puts it in *The Seasons of a Man's Life*:

- *'Only after we understand the profound significance of the epochs in our lives . . . can we understand the ways in which one is, at a single time, a child, a youth, a middle-aged and an elderly person. We are never ageless. As we gain a greater sense of our own biographies . . . we can begin to exist at multiple ages. In the process we do not fragment ourselves, rather we become more integrated and whole.'*

See how this might work for you by doing the following exercise.

> 1. Focus on yourself at a particularly stressful moment in your childhood. Really get into the image. Describe what you saw, where you were, what you looked like, who was with you, your thoughts, your feelings, and what you were doing.
>
> 2. Now ask your childhood self, 'Where are you hurting?' and 'What is troubling you?'
>
> 3. Now talk to your child and tell her or him that s/he will survive. Tell him or her what is going to happen, on the basis of what you know now. You can write it down or write your child a letter if you like.
>
> 4. Now think about any messages you have for the person you are now and say them out loud.

Doing this exercise enables you to gain a perspective on your life and to learn from your experiences so the past no longer has the same power to hurt you. By getting in touch with your inner child you come to recognise how you came to be the person you are today. The act of talking or writing to your inner child helps you to get in touch with the survivor part of your personality. In this way, you can choose healthy survival strategies in the future and change harmful patterns you may have developed as a result of your past. Of course, the bad things that happened to you will still remain but you can deprive them of the power to hurt you and learn to trust in your ability to look after yourself in the future.

RISKS AND RESOURCES

Survival has a lot to do with *when* particular experiences happen and the sorts of resources we have for dealing with them at that particular time in life. The degree of risk or protection we have from the bad things that can happen to us can often be traced back to other bad things that happened much earlier in our lives. For example, women whose mothers were absent (through death, separation or neglect) when they were children have been found to be more at risk of postnatal depression when they give birth themselves. However, it is possible to survive even if you are 'at risk' by making sure you are prepared for the challenges of parenthood and ensuring you have plenty of support from those around you. Having an absent mother in childhood can create a weakness which predisposes you to postnatal depression, but it is later events, such as lack of preparation for parenthood, a difficult birth or not having support, that create the risk. The lesson is that risk factors operate in different ways at different times. You can use this knowledge to take charge of your life and prepare yourself for important changes such as getting married or starting to live with your partner, starting or finishing work or having children.

When thinking about your own life tasks, it's important to bear in mind your past, present and future when deciding on survival strategies. Certain turning points can be particularly difficult. For example, if a parent died at 50 of an inherited condition, you may find your 50th birthday heralds a time of depresssion and uncertainty. Planning and preparation can help you to survive. You can read more about planning, preparation and the importance of setting goals in my companion book, *How To Get What You Want*.

TAKE A LIFE CHECK

The term life stages is used to describe the periods of time when we typically embark on particular life tasks. However, today age is becoming increasingly irrelevant as the timetable that guides our adult lives becomes more fluid. For example, some women have children in their teens, some wait until their 30s, 40s, or even, with the development of new birth technology, their 50s! Retirement ages are being abandoned and older people are working, taking up new careers or study, and doing a whole host of things that at one time would have been frowned upon.

Bearing all this in mind have a look at the following life stage timetable and ask yourself the following questions:

- What do I need to notice and reflect on at this stage in my life?
- What am I feeling?
- Are there any thoughts, emotions or feelings I need to act upon?
- What is my body telling me?
- Do I need to take a risk for future gain?

Review your life plan from time to time (say once a year) to make sure you are on course and to check for anything you need to change. The exact way in which you choose to deal with each stage, and the importance it has, depends, as always, on your individual values and beliefs. Bear in mind that the chronology of the various stages is approximate and that your personal timetable may well differ from others of the same age – you may leave home earlier than most of your friends, have children older, or face early retirement or redundancy. However, sooner or later, most of the life tasks have to be faced and if you don't deal with them at the time they usually crop up again later.

EXPERIMENTING IN LIVING: LATE TEENS/EARLY 20S

Life tasks: This is the time of your life when you are moving from the security of home and family towards increasing independence. It's a time for taking exams, going to college or university, starting your first job, or getting work experience. It's a time for fun and excitement: moving into your first apartment or studio, making new friends and relationships with the opposite sex, travelling and trying out different lifestyles and ways of behaving.

> How I am feeling ....
>
> Things I need to think about ....
>
> Things I can do..

PUTTING DOWN ROOTS: MID-20S TO MID-30S

Life tasks: At the beginning of this phase you may be busy training for or getting a career or job, buying your first apartment or house, firming up friendships, making friends in a new area or job. By your late 20s you may start asking 'Who am I?' and 'Where am I going?'. You may be ready to make a definite commitment such as getting married or moving in with a boyfriend or girlfriend, or change direction in life, work or relationships. You may be retraining for a new job or career, or undergoing divorce or separation from a long-term partner. By your early 30s, you may be recognised in your chosen field of work, promoted, moving ahead in your career, finding someone to help you in your career, or widening your scope if you have your own business or are freelance. You may be thinking about buying or moving house, or having your first child.

> How I am feeling ....
>
> Things I need to think about ....
>
> Things I can do..

IT'S NOW OR NEVER: MID-30S TO MID-50S

Life tasks: In the first of these two decades you may start asking 'Why am I doing this?' 'Is this all there is?' It's a time for making sense of time passing and growing older and facing the gap between who you are and who you wanted to be. In this phase, you are probably thinking about how you want to live the rest of your life. As a result, you may decide to make changes in your relationship, job or outside activities.

As you reach the second of the two decades you may begin to reorder your priorities, to let go of the struggle to succeed, to accept what you have. Your life tasks may include developing new coping strategies and interests, and achieving a better balance between work and leisure. If you have lost a partner or close friend you may return to some of the life tasks of your 20s.

> How I am feeling..
> Things I need to think about..
> Things I can do ....

FREEWHEELING: MID-50S ONWARDS

Life tasks: During the early part of this stage you may be thinking about when or if to retire, what to do and how to cope with the physical and mental changes of the next few years, taking on new activities and interests, coping with children growing up and/or leaving home, having grandchildren, and growing older. If you retire, you will be concerned with establishing a new identity for yourself. If you carry on working, you may be concerned to rearrange your working hours so you work less hard. It becomes important to spend time with people you want to spend time with. Now is often a time for questioning the meaning of life, re-evaluating your attitudes, passing on what you have learnt to others younger than you, and coming to terms with ageing and death.

> How I am feeling..
> Things I need to think about..
> Things I can do ....

If any of the turning points cause you particular difficulties, don't be afraid to seek help from other people. Counselling and psychotherapy can often help you change and transform yourself. Bear in mind the importance of looking after yourself as you pass through each life stage. Learning to trust in yourself and your ability to learn from your experiences and then leave them behind are the essence of the survivor personality. Looking for what you stand to gain from each new stage will help you deal with the loss of the previous one.

MAKING THE MOST OF TURNING POINTS

Turning points are times when you move from one life stage to the next, or times when you go through a particularly important experience, such as moving in with your partner or getting married, having a baby, or the break up of a relationship. Such times tend to throw into focus our life so far, so they are a great time for doing a life check and seeing whether your life is going in the direction you want it to go. Try to become aware of your turning points and use them to think about your life, decide to take a new direction, pay attention to dealing with things that happened in the past and generally hone your survivor skills.

Three vital questions:

1. **Do I need to change?** To answer this question you need to collect all the relevant information and 'facts' relating to the way you are now. Ways to gain knowledge include:

- Reading
- Talking to other people
- Making comparisons, considering the pros and cons, drawing conclusions

- Using your intuition
- Understanding the relevance of the knowledge you have gained

2. **Do I want to change?** To answer this you need to have a personal awareness of your experiences, feelings, values and attitudes to be able to see how they apply to the facts and information you have gathered. To gain this personal awareness:

- Think about what you have learned from reviewing your life experiences
- Think about what determines your attitudes towards your life
- Share your insights with others

3. **Do I have the confidence to change?** Your confidence in your ability to make the right decision for you and put that decision into practice will increase if you learn to make 'No-lose decisions'. Confidence comes from being aware of the skills you are building up and practising them.

Before....

- Focus on the idea that you will gain something – whatever happens. Push away thoughts of what you have to lose and concentrate instead on what you will gain.
- Talk to other people who can help you with the decision you are about to make, such as professionals in the field of a career move, other people who have made similar decisions, people you meet at parties, at the hairdresser's or at the dentist. However, avoid people who are discouraging or make you feel bad about yourself.
- If at first you don't succeed... Remember each time you do

something it takes you further along the way to where you want to be. There's no such thing as a 'false' start – just a start. OK, if it doesn't work out, pick yourself up, think about what you can do to make your plan more effective and then start again.
- Trust your 'hunches'. Even after you've done all your homework, talked to the people you need to talk to and come up with a logical choice, some inner voice may be propelling you to do something different. Don't ignore your inner voice. Sometimes you just have to follow your hunches – and you'll probably be surprised by how accurate they turn out to be.
- Learn to laugh. Hang on to your sense of humour – you'll need it. Most change involves a lot of ups and downs and if you can see the funny side of them you'll survive better

... And After

- Focus on the here and now. There's a wonderful scene in the movie *When Harry Met Sally*, when Sally learns her ex-partner is about to marry. Sally wails, 'But she was supposed to be his transitional person – she wasn't supposed to be *the one*.' The mental images we carry about how things are 'supposed' to be can be the cause of much unhappiness and deprive us of the chance to enjoy the way things are now. Mental images, as we've discovered, can be tremendously useful in helping us to project ourselves into the future and make decisions about the way we want to go. But once you have decided on a particular route, get rid of your preconceptions and concentrate on what is really happening. And don't forget to look for the 'gift'. What happens may be very different from the way you imagined it – but it can still be marvellous.
- Take responsibility for your decisions.

- Be flexible. If things don't work out the way you want them to – change your mind. By sticking with a decision we have made, even though we don't like the path we have taken, we prevent ourselves from learning and growing. You may attract criticism from other people: 'What do you mean you don't want to be a potter any more? You've spent the last four years at Art College. What a waste of time and money!' None of your training has gone to waste. It was the right thing for you to do at the time and you learned a lot and gained a lot of experience, but now it's not right for you any more. Remember – it's your life that is at stake.

How do you know if you are off course? Learn to listen to the inner clues, what your body is telling you: the migraines you inexplicably get every time you have to meet a certain person, the tension in your shoulders when you have to do a task you dislike, the still, small voice inside telling you that this course of action is wrong for you.

GOOD TIMES, BAD TIMES ROUND UP

You now have a good idea of the importance of time and how being aware of time enables you to stay in touch with what is going on with your life, so you can stay in charge.

- I am aware of the changes that have happened in my lifetime and can appreciate what I have gained and lost as a result
- I am aware of what stage of life I am in at present, which challenges I have already survived and which are still to come

> - I am prepared to survive life's challenges as they come along and confident that I can do so

Now you are ready to look at how to deal with specific events and turning points in Part Two.

PART TWO
MAKING IT WORK

CHAPTER SEVEN
SURVIVING A BREAK UP

Love, as we have already seen, is crucial to survival. Children who grow up safe in the knowledge that they are loved have a head start in the survival stakes (though even in families where parents were unloving, a child can still survive if s/he has someone who loves him or her). As adults, love is equally important: the presence of an intimate relationship in the form of a partner, relative or close friend, arms us against loneliness and depression. Equally, the break up of a relationship poses one of the biggest threats to survival.

THE TROUBLE WITH LOVE

The ancient Greeks had five words for love; we have only one. And that is part of the problem, because that one little word often means different things to different people and can change throughout a relationship. The trouble is that many of us attach unrealistic expectations to our relationships in the name of love. We enter into a permanent commitment at a time when we are blinded by our own needs. When we open our eyes, we may discover that our partner is unable or unwilling to meet those needs, and has needs of his or her own that we cannot satisfy. That's when the problems start, especially if you or your partner entered the relationship in the first place mainly to bolster a shaky sense of self esteem.

RELATIONSHIPS AND CHANGE

Like life, relationships are always moving on. Successful relationships are all about balance. Relationships – like survivors – have a self-righting tendency when change comes along. Often, after a period of readjustment, a new equilibrium is achieved. However, sometimes a relationship becomes so unbalanced during a period of change that it is unable to right itself. Some of the changes that can unbalance a relationship include:

- **A change in circumstances**
  The birth of a baby (however much planned and wanted), changes in your financial situation, a house move, job change, the illness of one partner, can all have repercussions on your relationship. Preparing for such changes with your partner can help you to weather them. However, sometimes the changes are so profound that the relationship never really recovers. For instance, if your relationship has always been based on you both being highly independent, and then one of you has to start leaning more on the other because of illness, say, this can be extremely stressful.

- **A change in you or your partner**
  As you pass through the various stages of life, it is inevitable that you will change. The person you are at 20 is very different to the person you are at 30, 40 and so on. The couple who troop down the aisle in their 20s will be very different to the couple cutting their silver wedding cake 25 years later. Sometimes you will both be changing at the same time: you may both decide you are ready to have children, for instance. However, often you will find that one of you is going through a time of change while the other one is standing still: you get promoted while your partner is feeling stuck in his or her career. Sometimes you may both be changing, but in different directions: you want to go back to college or

work, while your partner is reassessing his career and wanting to spend more time with the family. Liberal helpings of self-confidence, flexibility, support, problem-solving abilities, esteem and humour – in other words resilience – are necessary if the relationship is to survive.

- **Growing apart**

  However much you want your relationship to survive, sometimes you may both change so much that you grow apart. This is especially likely in couples who met and settled down very young. Sometimes a crisis, such as an affair, brings you up short and causes you to take a long, hard look at your relationship. Sometimes the process is so slow that you don't notice it, but one day you wake up and discover that you no longer have anything left in common.

RELATIONSHIPS IN TROUBLE

The problems that beset relationships are as varied as the couples in them and so are the signs that something is wrong. For some couples, the main sign that their relationship is on the rocky road to separation or divorce courts is the fact that they argue all the time without really ever getting anywhere. Others are good at papering over the cracks, while ignoring the rifts that lie underneath. They may never exchange an angry word; underneath, all the things that are tearing the relationship apart continue to fester. This may be because one partner is not aware enough or doesn't care enough to express their views. Other couples focus on the symptoms of a relationship in trouble – his affairs, her drinking, his hobby, the time she spends on her career – without ever really looking at why their partnership isn't working. However they manifest themselves, once problems have developed, there's a nagging sense of disillusion or dissatisfaction that sooner or later demands to be looked at.

UNDERSTANDING THE BREAK UP

Remember the cycle of change we looked at in Part One?

> Underawareness or denial
>
> Thinking about your options
>
> Preparation
>
> Action
>
> Maintaining the change

Relationship break ups follow much the same pattern. First of all comes the dawning reality that something is not quite right (stage one). You realise that Prince Charming isn't quite so charming after all, that your partner isn't who you thought he or she was or what you want him or her to be. At this stage you may feel so disappointed that you try to deny it. You 'make allowances', pretend you haven't noticed, or hope that your discoveries will go away. Sooner or later, however, you are forced to recognise the reality of the problems that have developed in your relationship. Sometimes, especially in short-lived relationships where you haven't much to lose, or in relationships in which you have been leading increasingly separate lives, the relationship make break up there and then, without either of you really understanding what went wrong or why.

However, in other relationships, especially where partners have a longer or deeper commitment, couples begin to acknowledge their problems (stage two) and may start to try and sort things out (stage three). At this stage, you may try to negotiate with each other by making deals such as, 'If you helped me more with the children, I wouldn't be too tired for sex,' or 'If you stopped spending so much of your time playing tennis, we would be able to spend more time together trying to work things out.' At this point, you may move into stage four: action. You may start trying to improve things by spending more time with the children or playing less tennis. This can sometimes help. However, unless the fundamental problem – that your partner is not who you want him or her to be – is tackled, the relationship continues to drift inexorably towards breakdown. Eventually, you may give up any hope of finding what you want from your relationship and decide either to separate or to carry on living together but to put less and less into the relationship.

This is not to say that a relationship in trouble cannot be saved. Real positive action in stages three and four can often pull couples on the verge of splitting up back from the brink. However, we are concentrating here on what happens in couples who do break up. If your relationship is in deep trouble, recognising that there is a predictable pattern enables you to prepare for splitting up, both emotionally and practically, in such a way that you both survive.

Stage five of the cycle of change, is about maintaining your gains. In the case of a relationship breakdown, that may mean recognising what went wrong and taking some time – either with your partner or on your own – working on this, so you don't run into the same problems next time. If you have children, it will probably mean working out how you both continue to be parents and meet your children's needs now you are apart. If you have chosen to remain friends, you need to spend some time drawing up the parameters of your changed relationship.

GIVING IT TIME

Bear in mind that the cycle of change rarely rolls completely smoothly. Most of us stumble through the various stages, only half aware of what is happening. Our feelings, thoughts and emotions often get in the way and prevent us from moving through the stages constructively. And many of us move towards parting and then pull back again many times before making a final decision. Accepting that this may happen will help you get through when all you can seem to see is arguments, confrontations and stalemate. Bear in mind that dealing with problems takes time. One reason is that both partners in a relationship are often on a different timetable. You may realise long before your partner that things are not right. But both you and your partner may be unwilling to face up to reality. And factors such as children, joint mortgages, shared friendships or work, low self-esteem and fear of the future can hamper you even further.

Taking things slowly and giving yourself and your partner time is not such a bad thing — however painful it may appear at the time — because it gives you the chance to adjust and to make sure that the relationship really is irretrievable. What isn't so beneficial is if, having acknowledged that things are going wrong, you let things drift without trying to deal with what is happening. Many relationships could have been saved if both partners had got used to using their emotional radar to detect times when the relationship was becoming unbalanced and taking action at an earlier stage.

THINKING ABOUT YOUR CHOICES

There are four options with any change. None of them is the right way for everyone, as much will depend on your and your partner's individual circumstances. It's very common for couples going through a relationship breakdown to try one or more of them.

- Option 1: live with it
  You may decide to let the relationship stay as it is and either do nothing and hope for the best or focus on other things outside the relationship such as your work or hobbies.
- Option 2: work on changing the relationship
  You may decide to address the problems in the relationship through negotiation, planning (remember to go for win/win solutions) and dealing with the issues underlying your problems. Professional relationship counselling can often help, especially where both partners are committed to the relationship and want to change it for the better.
- Option 3: work on changing yourself
  Another option is to change your own priorities and expectations with regard to the relationship. As a result, you may find that your attitude towards the relationship

changes and it either becomes more tolerable, or you decide it really is beyond repair and go on to option 4. As with option 2 it is often very helpful to do some work on yourself through psychotherapy or counselling.

- Option 4: abandon the relationship
  The final option is to decide that the relationship no longer has enough going for it to make it worthwhile and that you are going to leave it altogether. Your decision will be influenced by factors such as money, whether or not you have children, your age and life stage and so on. Some people try a trial separation, others split up and leave the relationship altogether.

TIME TO LEAVE?

Knowing when a relationship is over can be surprisingly difficult. No-one enjoys the pain of parting and for this reason many of us put off the evil moment for far too long. Use the following checklist to help you see whether you have explored all the possibilities:

- **Have you talked it over with each other?**
  Are you certain that you have honestly tried to get to the bottom of why the relationship isn't working, and listened (yes, really listened) to what your partner has to say? Remember, it can take time to start listening genuinely. You may need to go over and over the same ground before you feel that you are getting anywhere. If you are really stuck and unable to communicate, it can help to seek outside help from a counsellor or therapist.
- **Is the relationship really to blame?**
  Are you expecting your relationship to satisfy all your needs? It's unrealistic to expect your partner to satisfy your every need. Think about what is missing in your life and what changes you could make in yourself and your own life (see *How To Get What You Want*). Do your

problems stem from other stresses such as change of job, moving house, financial pressures, illness and so on? Or are you blaming your problems on these things rather than focussing on your ability to share and support each other through life's crises?

- **Are you confusing love with need?**
  If your relationship is truly over – your partner is deeply unhappy and wants to leave, is not prepared to work at it with you or is physically or emotionally abusing you – are you confusing your fear of independence and being alone with your desire to save it? If your partner really does want out – and is not just using it as a way of trying to get some sort of change in the relationship – it's better for both your happiness not to cling on. Remember: where there's a will there's a way, but where there is no will there is no way.

- **Have you talked over the situation with someone else?**
  Talking the situation over with a friend, relative or counsellor, or someone who is willing to listen to you but not take sides, can help you put the situation in perspective and enable you to explore various alternatives.

- **Are you acknowledging your own part in the relationship breakdown?**
  Are you aware of the way your own attitudes, thoughts and feelings have contributed to the present situation? It takes two to create a relationship and two to cause its downfall. Is there anything you could do to improve your relationship, such as going for counselling, talking to your partner, or negotiating? Do you really *want* to?

- **If you have a new relationship are you being realistic about the future?**
  It's all too easy in the first flush of a new relationship to imagine that you will be better off with your new partner than in a relationship that is bogged down by all the everyday pressures of life. If you are tempted to end a relationship for an affair, it is important to be scrupulously

honest about the needs the affair is serving. There are all sorts of reasons why someone is unfaithful – protest, insecurity, fear of growing older, excitement, fear of intimacy, sex, restlessness or a strong need to leave the relationship. Painful though it is, it is important to confront why it happened before rushing into the sunset with your new lover. If you don't, you could find yourself facing exactly the same choice sooner than you would wish.

- **Do you have the practical resources to part at this stage?** Have you prepared yourself practically for separation? Is there anything you need to do in order to separate, e.g. get a job, find somewhere to live, sort out finances, childcare and so on? If you are in a violent or abusive relationship, you may need to find a shelter.

Another way of deciding is to do what is called a cost-benefit analysis, in which you list the things you will lose and the things you will gain by going or staying.

Having answered these questions you may find you are sure that you want to end the relationship, or you may feel it's worth exploring some of these avenues to see if you can find some solutions. It takes time to come to a decision and you can expect to experience a great deal of uncertainty about whether you are doing the right thing. If you do decide to separate, both you, your partner and any children you have, will survive better if you can prepare.

POWER GAMES

All relationships involve mutual dependency. In a healthy relationship, however, each partner is able to support and be supported without being exploited. Toxic relationships involve an imbalance in dependency. One partner over-invests time, emotions, money, often in a vain attempt to satisfy their need for love. Such a relationship is often deeply unbalanced and/or abusive, with the other partner controlling the relationship. In such a relationship fear of how your partner will respond can keep you paralysed.

And, as you know by now, action is the essence of survival. Understanding what is going on can often be a first step towards making a plan of action and beginning to take control. If you are in an abusive relationship, use the following checklist to help you recognise what is going on:

> - My partner constantly criticises me and accuses me of 'mistakes'
> - My partner controls me through moods, anger and threats
> - My partner overprotects and 'cares' for me
> - My partner rubbishes my thoughts and opinions
> - My partner ignores my needs
> - My partner makes all the decisions
> - My partner controls our finances
> - My partner blames me for everything that goes wrong
> - My partner doesn't like me to spend time with other people
> - My partner physically intimidates me
> - My partner sexually humiliates me
> - My partner is physically or sexually violent

It can be especially hard to leave a relationship of this kind, because all your energies will be concentrated simply on surviving. It's very important not to blame yourself, and to bear in mind that you are not alone. You can change your life, but it may take time. Use the suggestions in this chapter and throughout this book to gather your strength and make sure you have a good support network to help you gain the courage and practical resources you will need. Many people who have left such relationships find that they gain tremendous strength and resilience simply from having survived, which helps them in their future lives.

ACKNOWLEDGING YOUR FEELINGS

As with any loss, the ending of a relationship leads to a profound sense of grief and a period of mourning. The stages of grief are similar to the stages of change discussed elsewhere. At first, you can expect to experience shock and denial – 'This can't be happening'. The next stage may involve a great deal of anger and guilt – 'How could you, after all I've done for you?' or 'If only I hadn't done such and such, the relationship wouldn't have broken down.' The third stage of grief often includes bargaining and negotiating with your partner to try and keep the relationship going. For instance. 'Can you come over and fix my car and I'll cook you dinner?' Finally, the reality of the break up sinks in and you become extremely sad or even depressed. As with any change, it's common to move backwards and forwards through these stages.

It takes time – and courage – to get over the loss of an important relationship. How you cope will owe much to way in which you have handled previous losses. Unhealed grief about losses from your past can rear its head at this time, making it hard to acknowledge your feelings of sadness, anger, guilt and so on. This can lead to you denying your feelings, for example by throwing yourself into a frantic round of work or socialising. Alternatively, you may become stuck at a particular stage in your grief. You may find yourself doing things which may be harmful in the long run, such as preventing your partner from seeing the children, getting involved in lengthy and expensive litigation, making excuses to see your ex-lover, and so on. Remaining stuck can also lead you to sabotage future relationships by bringing your emotional luggage with you. If you are finding it hard to let go, there may be some deeply buried grief from your past which is obstructing you. Talking to a counsellor who can help you uncover what it is that is blocking your grief by doing some 'grief work' can help you to let go and move on.

WAYS TO HELP

- Continue talking to your partner. However upsetting it is, talking can provide you with insights into the relationship and each other, even if it has to end. Talking about the decisions you have made together about the future is important too, especially if you have children.
- Be honest with each other. Acknowledge that it is difficult and that your emotions can lead you to behave in a hurtful way at times. If your emotions prevent you from making any progress, stop the discussion and try again later. Have a look at Chapter Three for information on how to deal with powerful feelings. When you do try to discuss things with each other, concentrate on telling your partner exactly how you feel without accusation or blame. Use what is called 'I' language. For example, 'When you do . . . I feel . . .', rather than 'You make me feel . . .' Accusation and blaming are ways of avoiding responsibility and lead to feelings of helplessness or anger which can keep you stuck.
- Take responsibility for your own emotions. Accept your emotions and recognise that it's natural for them to fluctuate. Allow yourself to express your feelings, to cry, to shout, to be angry and sad (see Chapter Three). If you are the one who is leaving, guilt may be your main emotion. Remind yourself that you are trying to deal with your break up as best you can. If you are stuck in anger, sadness or guilt, it can sometimes help you to imagine how your partner is feeling. This can help you to understand that s/he has lost something too and shift you from where you are stuck.
- Find yourself some support. Talk to friends about how you are feeling (see Chapter Four). Don't be tempted to rush straight into a new relationship to heal the pain of this one. Love on the rebound often works for a time. However, unless you have addressed the real issues involved, you may find yourself facing uncannily familiar problems in the

new relationship. Instead, work on your existing friendships. Join a group. Find a counsellor or therapist.
- Get the practicalities sorted out. If you are divorcing or there are legal aspects of your relationship to disentangle, such as joint ownership of a house, car or business, find out what you have to do to sort them out. Get a book or seek advice from a lawyer or advice centre. If you do decide to appoint a lawyer, try not to become embroiled in legal battles with your partner. Mutual co-operation works best, especially if there are children involved. The only person to profit from continued battles with your partner is your lawyer.
- Go easy on yourself. You are responsible for your own feelings and actions but you are only responsible up to a point for how your partner deals with the break up. If you have children, of course you have an emotional, practical and legal responsibility towards them. Both you and your partner have responsibility for your own feelings. Recognise what s/he is feeling and talk about it, but don't allow yourself to be drawn into continuing the relationship in other ways – for example, by constant arguing over the 'phone – once you have made the decision that it has truly ended.
- Recognise that it is safe to let go of your feelings. Allowing yourself to let go is vital, so you can heal and then move on. Allowing yourself to heal doesn't have to mean getting back with your partner, unless of course you both want to. Meditation and the technique called visualisation can help. Another powerful way of letting go of your feelings is to write them down in a diary or in letters. It can help to write a letter to your partner. At first this may be real 'hate mail' – do not be tempted to post this. Your eventual aim should be to produce a letter which describes your feelings in a non-blaming way, and acknowledges both the negative and positive aspects of your lost relationship. This letter should be one that you would feel good about receiving yourself. You can choose whether or not to post this.

Remember: it takes two to make a relationship. A relationship can't exist just because you want it to or think it ought to: it can't exist either just because your partner wants it to. Continuing honesty about your feelings will enable you both to accept that the relationship has ended.

WHAT ABOUT THE CHILDREN?

There's no doubt that most, if not all, children find a relationship break up traumatic. Research has shown that even ten years after their parents' break up, many children still have painful memories. However, recent research has shown that it's not all bad news: children can actually benefit from the ending of a stormy relationship if it reduces the stress they are experiencing and frees either or both parents to be more sensitive and responsive to their needs. In fact, some children thrive after a divorce or separation. You can help your children to survive and thrive by paying attention to the following:

- **Keep them in the picture**
  Many parents, usually because of their own hurt and confusion, fail to tell their children what is going on. This results in much pain and anxiety. Children are able to sense that something is wrong, even if you don't tell them. However, if they aren't allowed to 'know' they may bottle up their own feelings of distress and pain. And, as you have discovered, suppressing feelings is harmful to the development of a survivor personality. When my ex-partner and I were thinking about splitting up but hadn't yet decided upon it and therefore hadn't told our children, my eldest daughter, who was then 11, put a big notice in her bedroom, 'Divorce is worse than nuclear war' – a poignant and all too painful reminder that she was aware of the situation even though we hadn't told her. However painful you find it, it's important to explain to your children what is happening in terms that they can understand. Young

children in particular can often fear that something they did was responsible for the break up. It's important to emphasise that your decision is something you have decided, that it is not their fault, and that there is nothing to do to alter it.

- **Pick the right time**
Take into account your child's age and stage of development when deciding when to tell them. The older your child, the more time s/he needs to get used to the idea. Researchers suggest that older children can be told more or less as soon as you know yourself, five- to eight-year-olds a month or two before, and under-fives a week or two before you make the break. Allow your children to ask questions and encourage them to talk about their childhood, perhaps with the aid of photograph albums or stories about when they were little, so they can see the good as well as the bad things that came out of your relationship.

- **Allow them to express their feelings**
Your children need to grieve just as much as you do, however painful this may be for you. You can support your children as they mourn by acknowledging your own grief, talking to them and allowing them to express their feelings in their own way and in their own time. It's common for children to revert to an earlier stage of development, for example to start wetting the bed, to play up at school, to be angry or to indulge in 'magical' thoughts that you will get back together again. You will need all your strength to help your children to accept the truth and support them in their grief. Research has shown that allowing children to grieve and supporting them through it helps to build resilience in later life. By contrast, children who have not been encouraged to express their grief have a higher incidence of depression in later life.

- **Encourage them to get support from other people**
Children need to realise that, although sad, family breakdown is normal and nothing to be ashamed of. After all one in five children lose a parent through divorce or

separation. Let them know that it is alright by you if they confide in their friends, grandparents, teachers, friends' parents and other supportive adults. Emotional support from outside the family can do much to help your children to adjust to your separation. In some cases, it may help them to talk to a therapist who is experienced in dealing with children.

- **Help them to feel some control**

  One of the worst things about a divorce or separation from a child's point of view is the lack of control they may feel over their own lives. You can help your children to feel more in control by listening to them, allowing them to express their feelings about practical arrangements regarding contact with their other parent, and in making joint decisions about matters that affect them like outings, birthday parties, holidays and treats. At the same time, however, they should not feel that they are having to make major decisions such as choosing between you.

- **Don't use your children as go-betweens or pawns**

  Resist at all costs the temptation to involve your children in on going struggles with your partner. Don't pressurise them to take sides and if your feelings are so strong that you are unable to control your anger, explain to your children that you say things that you don't mean when you are angry. Don't use your children as spies to find out if your partner has someone else, or details of your partner's new relationship. It can be tempting if you resent your partner's new relationship to encourage them to put down his or her new partner. However, you will be doing your children – and yourself – no favours in the long run. Try to see your ex's new partner as an addition to your children's lives, rather than a replacement, and encourage them to do likewise.

- **Try to minimise other sources of disruption**

  Divorce and separation often bring a whole host of other stressful changes such as changing schools, moving house, court hearings and so on. It's much easier for children – as it is for anyone – to deal with one or two stresses rather than a whole lot all at once. Some changes may be unavoidable. However, try to avoid piling change upon change, and perhaps plan to delay some changes such as moving, until the child has had time to adjust to your separation.

- **Show them you love them**
  Both you and your partner need to make it clear to your children that you still love them and care for them, no matter what. Read Chapter Three and don't be afraid to hug your children and show them that you still love them.

SURVIVING A BREAK UP ROUNDUP

A relationship break up is one of the most stressful and painful experiences any of us go through and it calls for all our survivor qualities. You'll know that you have truly survived when you can honestly tick all the boxes below:

- I can appreciate the good and bad aspects of my former relationship

- I do not blame my ex-partner for our break up

- I can accept that although our break up was painful, it was for the best

- I do not dwell on what my ex-partner is doing with his or her life

- I can allow my children to enjoy spending time with my ex-partner

- I am interested in what my children tell me about my ex-partner, but I do not feel a need to pry

> - I feel OK talking to my ex-partner and neither seek excuses to contact him/her unnecessarily or to avoid contact
> - I feel confident about entering a new relationship without undue caution

Yes? If you have ticked all, or most, of the above, then you are well on your way to recovery – and survival. Well done! If you haven't, don't worry, give it time and carry on working on the points raised in this chapter.

CHAPTER EIGHT
SURVIVING JOB LOSS

Time was when most of us expected to have a job with good pay, regular holidays, and a nice fat pension at the end of it all. In a stable world, work was a source of security, status and a sense of identity. Today, all that has changed. Few people these days work the proverbial 'nine-to-five' day and short-term contracts, projects, part-time or temporary work and self-employment are the order of the day. In fact, these days most people can expect to change job or career several times.

Getting promoted, taking another step up the career ladder, changing jobs or losing your job because you have resigned or been made redundant or dismissed, all call for survival tactics. The cycle of change applies to work and to any other sort of change. Remember the five stages?

> Underawareness or denial
>
> Thinking about your options
>
> Preparation
>
> Action
>
> Maintaining the change

CAREER MOVES

A change in your working situation can come about for many different reasons. You yourself may have decided that it is time for a change. You may feel you are no longer being stretched in your present work. Your job may have changed and become less satisfying. You may have decided you want or need more money, perhaps because you are planning to start a family, want to travel or buy a house. Or perhaps you want a move because you realise promotion prospects in your existing job are slim.

Change may be being imposed upon you. You may sense that your job may not be yours for much longer. Perhaps you no longer have the qualifications and skills needed and fear being made redundant. Perhaps you started off dealing mainly with people – customers or staff – but as you have progressed or the firm has grown bigger, your work has changed and now involves analytical or technological skills, which you don't possess or feel comfortable with. Perhaps your firm is merging with another or faced with the threat of complete closure. Alternatively, you may be coming up to retirement age, or decide to take early retirement because you can afford to do so, or for some other reason such as illness.

Whatever the reason for change, your survival depends on feeling that you are in charge of your own life and the degree to which you are able to prepare for it.

SHOULD I GO OR SHOULD I STAY?

If you decide to change job, you will be in a slightly stronger position than someone who is dismissed or made redundant. Even so, careful preparation is vital to ensure that you find work that satisfies you better than the job you are in at present. The first glimmer of change may be feeling bored or not challenged by your job. The hours seem to tick by more slowly than they once did, you find yourself wondering when it is lunchtime and looking at your watch or the clock to see whether it is time to go home yet. You have less enthusiasm when you are asked to do a particular task or work overtime. Sooner or later, the realisation hits you that it is time to make a change. The following checklist can help you to start focussing on whether your present job is fulfilling your needs.

> Tick the ones that apply to you:
> - I don't feel my qualifications and experience are being used to the full
> - I feel I could earn more by moving to another job
> - The prospects of promotion in my present job look slim
> - I want the challenge of doing something new
> - I feel if I don't move now I never will
> - I am ready for a change of direction

The next step is to start making preparations for a change by considering your qualifications and experience and thinking about whether you may have any transferable skills (see the companion to this book, *How To Get What You Want*, for a fuller discussion of this) or whether you need to update your skills and qualifications. You'll need to think about your chances of moving: staying too long in one job these days often isn't seen as a good thing. You also need to check your personality and your personal circumstances. Do you enjoy change and the challenge of doing something new? How old are you? It can be difficult to make a move after 45. And how would your family react to your changing course and possibly having to move?

WHAT NEXT?

Most people who are contemplating a career move imagine they are looking for a dramatic change. In fact, research has shown that nine out of ten career changes are actually adjustments. Whatever we may imagine, we are not in the field we are in by accident. In fact, many of us like more aspects of the job we do than we realise. The urge to do something different may be fuelled by dissatisfaction with pay, benefits or hours rather than the job itself. Career changes can't be accomplished overnight, so give yourself time and allow yourself to dream. Your enthusiasm and desire to do something different can give you the energy to navigate your way through the lottery of job searches.

SURVIVING JOB LOSS
PREPARING FOR JOB LOSS

Of course, your impending job change may not be voluntary. Yet despite the horror stories we have all heard about people going in to work and being told to clear their desk before lunchtime, job loss rarely comes completely out of the blue. A key survival skill is to tap into your intuition so as to spot the straws in the wind. There are no hard and fast rules but according to career specialists Godfrey Golzen and Philip Plumbley, signs that you could be in a vulnerable position include:

- You hold a senior position in a company that is being taken over (especially if you were loudly opposed to the takeover)
- Your company has merged with another company in the same field
- A division or overseas office in your organisation is being closed down, even if you aren't directly working in those parts of the organisation
- Your firm or company is losing profits or the profit margin is closing, especially during times of general economic pressure. Such a record can lead to 'rationalisation' of staff as well as resources
- Your boss or someone with whom you have been working closely has been dismissed, removed or transferred
- You are allocated to an assignment or project that is clearly streets away from where the action is

- You face unexpected delays and obstacles when trying to get money to spend on staff or equipment
- You stop being asked to key meetings that you would once have been asked to attend, especially if a colleague is now asked in your place
- You are not consulted about appointments of people below you, who you would normally expect to have interviewed and vetted

If you have spotted the writing on the wall, now is the time to put into practice all the skills you have learnt in controlling your emotions. Now is not the time to jeopardise your present job – or prospects of a redundancy settlement – by flouncing out in tears or temper! However humiliating and frustrating your present situation, it's important to bide your time. Confide in your partner or friends, rather than your boss, colleagues or the people under you. In the meantime, start searching for another job as hard as you can. Try not to panic and take anything you can get. Go about your job search calmly and methodically bearing in mind what you want.

COPING WITH JOB LOSS

If you have already been made redundant, resigned or been dismissed, you now have to face a period without a job. No-one can tell you how long you are going to be out of work. However, as with any loss, it is important to grieve. Work forms a central part of life for most of us and unemployment can come as a big blow to the confidence. It helps to remember that it is rarely your fault: work is changing rapidly and few people today can be entirely sure of their jobs.

The stages of grief apply just as much to job loss as they do to any kind of loss. At first, you will probably feel shocked and numb. This may be combined with a feeling of relief and even euphoria, especially if you have been unhappy for any length of time. After this, there may come a period of anger and resentment at your employers and yourself for not having realised what was on the cards, combined with fear that you may not get another job. There may also be guilt. You may believe that if you had done or not done something you would not have lost your job. You may feel desperately sad and lost, feeling as if you have lost part of yourself. The last stage of the process involves coming to terms with the fact that you have lost your job, accepting it, and starting to get down to the practical tasks of looking for another job. Finally, you may come to believe that losing your job was 'the best thing that ever happened to you.' Give yourself time and bear in mind that the grief process is more often like a whirlpool than a straightforward progression. Expect to dip in and out of the various phases, particularly at vulnerable points such as being called for an interview and then failing to get the job. The following tips can help you deal with the emotional challenges of losing your job:

- **Get rid of outdated ideas about losing a job**
  Dismiss from your mind any embarrassment about being made redundant and don't blame yourself. These days, job flexibility is the norm. You have nothing to be ashamed of and you have no need to be apologetic or defensive when talking about your situation.
- **Face the facts**
  Realise that, unless you are exceptionally lucky, employers are not going to be queuing up for your services. You will have to work at finding employment. Write a detailed description of all your skills and talents and the things you do well. Describe specific projects or assignments that you feel especially proud of. Describe your people skills, or your skills with computers or equipment. Give yourself a big pat on the back. Now analyse what you have written to see what you have to offer to prospective employers and where there are any gaps that need attention (see *How To Get What You Want* for more on this subject).
- **Practise talking about your reliable strengths**
  Describe your abilities to a friend. You are going to need to be able to sell yourself in your search for a job, so get into practice.

- **Express how you feel**
  Talk to family, friends and colleagues about your job loss. If that isn't possible, try writing down your feelings about what has happened. Include anything you would like to have said to your employers – but didn't. It's important to leave behind any emotional baggage and resentments from your last job. They can weigh you down and make it harder for you to obtain employment. US psychologist James Pennebaker asked one group of unemployed people to write down their feelings about losing their jobs for 20 minutes over a period of five days. Another group were asked to write about time management for the same amount of time. Astonishingly he discovered that more of those who had written down their feelings about losing their jobs obtained further employment. You might find this exercise helpful too.

- **Get some support**
  Support is just as important when you have undergone job loss as it is for any other kind of loss. Find out the names of other people who are in a similar situation (there may be some who were laid off at the same time as you, you may have friends in a similar position, or you may meet people at a job club or outplacement agency). Keep in regular touch by telephone. As US psychologists Barbara Sher and Annie Gotlieb point out, we tend to have more courage for each other than we have for ourselves. Hold brainstorming sessions and help each other to discover opportunities.

MAKE FINDING A JOB YOUR NEW JOB

Get out and talk to people. Start 'phoning consultants, agencies, employers and any other contacts in the field in which you are seeking work. Bear in mind that nine out of ten job openings are never advertised. Make appointments, gather information, find out what's happening in firms where you want to work. Keep an eye out for new developments that could signal job opportunities. Scour the press and trade papers for news of:

- New products or services
- New firms moving into your area/market
- Staff changes
- Firms which have been offered new contracts
- Mergers and takeovers
- Relocations

The following tips may help in your search for work:

- **Don't waste time**
  Don't hang about the house as if you were on holiday. Set aside a certain number of hours a day for your search and stick to them. And bear in mind that the time scale of future employers is different from yours. Research shows that after 35 it takes on average six to nine months to find a new job. If you are 45 or over, it can take even longer. So start today and be prepared to be realistic.
- **Be persistent**
  Research has shown that a 'volume approach', contacting as many potential employers as possible, is the route to success. However, make sure you are contacting the right person in a firm or organisation. Target your letters, rather than just firing off a load of standard CVs. Find out who you need to write to by 'phoning the firm or company and asking for the name of the relevant person. Offer a bait to grab the interest of the person you are writing to but don't lay all your skills and talents on the line. Suggest going to see them to discuss prospects rather than begging for a job.
- **Focus on each employer's needs and think about how you can meet them**
  Only your cousin is going to hire you because you need a job, so you need to do some research on what is required for each job you apply for. Then customise your CV or application form to fit. Remember, survivors are adaptable.

Your future employer must be convinced that you are uniquely qualified for the job.

- **Before an interview take some time to meditate on your successes and skills**

  If you become bogged down by thoughts of all the times you have been turned down, you will not be in the right frame of mind to get a job. Read the section on changing your thoughts and developing a more positive outlook in Part One and then spend some time getting yourself into a winning frame of mind. The belief that an employer will be lucky to take you on will take you far.

- **Keep your eyes and ears open for opportunities**

  Talk to people you meet at home, while socialising, in a bus queue, or at the library. Ask them about what they are doing. You never know when an unexpected job opportunity is going to present itself.

- **Earn while you wait**

  If you haven't been given a big pay-off, or you got nothing, you may have to find temporary or short-term contract work. Aim for something close to the sort of job you have just left. Taking a job that under-uses your skills is bad for your confidence. However, be realistic. In fact, taking a job at a slightly lower level often goes down well, especially with small firms, where everyone lends a hand with everything.

- **Rebuild your self-esteem**

  See the section on self-esteem in Part One and make a list of all the things you like and appreciate about yourself and all the successes you have had in the past year – no matter how small. Another good way to boost your self-esteem is to obtain references or letters of appreciation from people you have worked with (be brave and ask for them if they aren't automatically forthcoming). As well as being useful for showing to future employers, they will help remind you of what a valuable contribution you have made.

- **Look after yourself**

Make sure you eat well, sleep well and get enough exercise and relaxation. (See *How To Get What You Want.*) Don't cut yourself off. Talk to your friends and family about what has happened, and if necessary seek professional counselling.

HOW TO SURVIVE AN INTERVIEW

Whatever job you go for, you will usually be required to attend an interview (formal or informal). This can call on all your survival skills. Good preparation is the key to surviving interviews.

▬ Before the interview:

- Find out as much as you can about the organisation or company in question and also about the person or people who are to interview you (ask your contacts, find people who work for the organisation, or look in professional directories where relevant)
- Prepare answers to obvious questions and expect to be asked questions about your family and, if you are a woman, what provisions you have made for childcare (I know it's sexist, but such questions still get asked so it's as well to be prepared with the answers)
- Summarise the main points of your CV, the job advert and any questions you have on a 'crib' card which you can refer to on your way to the interview or before being called in
- Practise the interview beforehand with a friend to help you prepare for any difficult questions or to overcome your fear of interviews
- Dress appropriately for the type of job you are applying for

▬ During the interview

- Bear in mind the structure of an interview. It's very like a meeting – the opening pleasantries, followed by a gentle start, more detailed probing and then a conclusion

- Use your empathy skills to assess the type of person your interviewer is and the style of questioning s/he is using. Think carefully before you answer questions and avoid either long silences or gabbling
- Think about when to introduce the main points you want to get across. The main points will be on your CV or application form. Select what you say and when to say it
- Do not lose your temper even if you feel the interviewer is offensive
- Be positive about your present or previous job and don't try to score points by making unpleasant remarks about your present or previous employers
- Be prepared for 'problem' questions. Think beforehand what they are likely to be (your homework will have helped here). If you are asked a problem question, stay calm an express yourself clearly and logically
- Be prepared with a list of relevant questions to ask at the end of the interview or as the occasion arises
- Think positively and challenge any negative thoughts. Remember you are not on trial – both you and the interviewer are equal. You want to know if what s/he has to offer is what you want, just as much as vice versa. And even if you don't get this job, it doesn't mean that you will never get a job.

After the interview:

- Try to avoid lengthy post-mortems. If the interview went badly, think about what went wrong and how you can make a better impression next time
- If the interview went well, you may be waiting anxiously for the post. If you do get the job, great. If you don't, remember it wasn't necessarily your fault

SURVIVING JOB LOSS ROUNDUP

- I can understand why I lost my job and the factors – both personal and in the work environment – that led up to it
- I can appreciate the good and bad aspects of my previous job
- I can accept that, although it was difficult losing my job, I have made some positive gains
- I am looking towards my future with confidence

Yes? If you have ticked all, or most, of the above then you have managed to survive the loss of your job successfully.

CHAPTER NINE
SURVIVING SICKNESS

One of the biggest challenges to our capacity to survive is illness, whether of the body or of the mind. In recent years, there has been a growing recognition that illness doesn't just affect the part of the body diagnosed as sick. Even physical illness also reflects your mental, emotional and, some would say, your spiritual state. In the past, conventional doctors have tended to take a rather 'nuts and bolts' approach to illness, concentrating on treating the physical symptoms and ignoring these other dimensions. Today, however, even orthodox doctors are beginning to take more of an interest in 'holistic' health – looking at the whole sick person rather than just his or her symptoms. This has come about partly in response to pressure from patients, who have been increasingly turning to complementary and alternative medicine, which differs from the orthodox approach in that it aims to uncover the underlying cause of the illness.

In this chapter, you will find out how to survive changes in health, whether they are voluntary or involuntary. You will find advice on how to cope with progressive or chronic illness and what you can do if you are told that you will die of your illness. These aren't easy matters to deal with and what I have written here is by no means the last word. As always, to survive you need to take charge of your life, something that can be especially hard when you are feeling physically weak. There may be times when all you want to do is hand over your body to the experts, and if that is the way you feel, fine. That is your positive choice. At other times, you may feel unhappy with your medical treatment. Remember that, though there is much that doctors and medical staff can do to help you, you know yourself better than anyone else: it's your body and your life.

Note: The ideas you will find in this chapter are not intended as prescriptions or medical advice, nor are they intended to replace specific advice given to you by your doctor or health practitioner.

YOUR HEALTH: WHOSE CHOICE?

The first thing to do in taking charge is to find ways of understanding the change that has come about. In many ways, we choose to be healthy just as much as we choose anything else in our lives. If you choose to neglect your body or treat it badly by driving it too hard, filling it with unwholesome food, or abusing it with cigarettes, too much alcohol or drugs, then it will be less likely to be able to support you if illness strikes. Of course, there are some things we can't change. Luck does come into it. We may have been born with a faulty gene or get sick, no matter how well we have looked after ourselves. In such circumstances, all we can do is support and care for our bodies and our minds so that the healing process can take place. The good news is that it's never too late to start caring for yourself and thinking about your health. Changes in health usually happen in three different ways:

- **Changes you have decided to make**

    You may have decided to pay attention to your health, sometimes out of a desire to be healthier, or sometimes as the result of a sudden glimpse of your own mortality. For instance, I stopped smoking overnight when my mother was diagnosed with cancer, even though my boyfriend of the time had just bought me a fancy cigarette lighter! Other positive health changes can be making sure you get enough sleep, watching what you eat, losing weight, taking up exercise and learning to relax. We have already looked at many of these in Chapter Two.

- **Involuntary change in health through accident or illness**
  These are changes in health that happen suddenly as a result of accident or illness. The effects of these can be either temporary (doctors usually refer to illnesses that come on suddenly and go away after a short period of time as acute illnesses) or permanent.
- **Progressive or chronic illness**
  These are illnesses or conditions such as diabetes, asthma, epilepsy or thyroid disease which will not go away. Doctors call such conditions chronic. Some of these conditions may keep changing for the worse; examples may be multiple sclerosis, cancer and heart disease. Such progressive conditions may eventually become so severe that they end your life. Doctors call these terminal. However, having a terminal illness doesn't necessarily mean that you are going to die tomorrow. Even so, being told you have such an illness is usually a terrible blow that can challenge all your survival skills.

A QUESTION OF BALANCE

One of the choices we have available today that wasn't available a few years ago is whether to seek treatment from an orthodox or alternative practitioner. Often it is possible to combine both orthodox and alternative therapy, and in this case the term complementary medicine is used. Although complementary is often used interchangeably with alternative, either orthodox medicine or alternative medicine can be complementary. The point is that they are being used *alongside* each other. In recent years there has been something of a swing away from modern orthodox medicine with its high-tech tests, treatments and strong drugs. This is not entirely justified, because when modern medicine does work well it often works very well indeed.

However, it's been estimated that eight out of ten of the illnesses we suffer from today are self-limiting; that is, they go away on their own without any treatment, or cannot be treated by modern high-tech medicine or surgery. Things which orthodox medicine does treat well include: serious or life-threatening illnesses or emergencies, injuries, acute infections caused by bacteria or viruses, tropical diseases, illnesses caused by parasites, mechanical breakdown or acute mental breakdown or psychiatric problems. What it doesn't do so well with and even treats badly are: problems affecting the bones and muscles that come and go such as backache, or arthritis, recurrent painful conditions such as headaches, migraines and sciatica, recurring infections such as cystitis and bronchitis, allergies, problems affecting the heart and circulation such as high blood pressure, problems affecting the nervous system such as multiple sclerosis, sleep disorders such as insomnia and chronic fatigue, anxiety, depression and the whole host of stress-linked illnesses and conditions. If you have one of these conditions, it may be worth deciding to visit an alternative practitioner. One of the biggest benefits of visiting an alternative practitioner, especially for chronic conditions (ones that don't go away), is that it can help you feel more in control of your body and your illness – an important factor in survival.

YOUR ILLNESS: BEING IN CONTROL

HANDLING YOUR EMOTIONS

All illnesses, even coughs and colds, involve emotions. In the case of a minor illness such as a cold, it may simply be irritation at having to stay off work or missing a social event you were looking forward to. With more serious illnesses the emotions are, of course, deeper and more difficult to deal with. It's common, as we have seen with other types of change, to deny at first that the illness is happening you, perhaps in the belief that by ignoring it, it will go away. If the sick person is a partner or close friend you may also deny or ignore it at first. When my daughter developed anorexia aged 17, at first I ignored what was happening. First of all, I couldn't believe that was what it really was, and then I think I hoped that it would go away of its own accord if I didn't 'make a big thing of it'.

Burying or suppressing your feelings won't, of course, make the illness disappear, though it may be a protective mechanism in the short term. However, keeping on denying your feelings can make it difficult to get the help you need, take positive action, which could put you in charge, and can lead to the development of depression (often a result of suppressing feelings). You will survive better if you give yourself time to accept your illness and not to expect too much of yourself. Keep on using the suggestions in Chapter Two to help you to get in touch with the feelings you are experiencing. Two exercises that can help put you in touch with your feelings about your illness follow. You will need a pen and paper, some time and two cushions.

> 1. Write a letter to your illness, describe how it feels to you, how it looks, how it sounds, how it affects you. Go into as much detail as you can. Now write your illness's reply to you in the same amount of detail. Now read the two letters. What feelings do they arouse? Write them down. Don't try to change your feelings at this stage, simply accept them for what they are as you learnt to do in Chapter Three.
>
> 2. First sit on one cushion, imagine that your illness or your body is sitting on the other cushion and talk to it. Now change places and take the part of your body or your illness and reply to what you have said. What does this say about you and your feelings? One woman who suffered bulimia said to her imaginary body, 'I hate you.' When she became her body she started to cry and said, 'Why don't you love me? I am beautiful and I have looked after you well.' This released such a deep feeling of sadness that from that moment on she was able to start being kinder to herself and stop abusing her body.

GET WISE TO YOUR ILLNESS

One of the worst things about falling sick is the feeling of being out of control, even when medically the doctor perceives treatment to be proceeding well. Knowledge is power; having knowledge can allow you to understand what the doctors tell you and to be an active participant in your treatment, a vital survivor skill, as it gives you back the feeling of control. Here are some things you can do:

- Acknowledge that you are ill. Talk about your illness to your family and friends, or if someone else has become ill, talk about their illness with them. Don't imagine that you are protecting the person by avoiding the subject – it will be on their mind whether you bring it up or not.
- Find out as much as you can about your illness. Find out what books have been written, read articles in magazines, go to your local library and find out if there is a medical database you can use.
- If you have a chronic illness or condition, find out if there is a support group for people with it. There are such groups for most major conditions and many less well-known ones these days. Meeting other people in a similar situation and learning how they have coped can help you feel less isolated.

DEALING WITH DOCTORS

Relationships are just as important in illness as they are in any other area of life. One of the main relationships you have when you fall sick is the relationship with your doctor. The doctor/patient relationship is not always an easy one. However, it's well worth working at it because it can affect your survival. One of the problems for doctors is lack of time. Another is that they have a different way of thinking about illness. A third is that the doctor/patient relationship has traditionally been one of power: the doctor's. Today, all that is changing as more and more of us develop survivor qualities.

However, you may still come across doctors who think they know best, who refuse to tell you about the drugs they have prescribed and their side effects, or who lie to you about your prognosis or are evasive – often in the mistaken knowledge that they are protecting you. Of course, doctors don't have it easy. Some people who are seriously ill cannot take or do not always want to know the complete truth. As with other relationships the answer is empathy. In a good doctor/patient relationship, your doctor will be prepared to answer your questions and will be able to sense whether you are ready to take the information he or she has about your illness.

The relationship between a doctor and a patient is a two-way contract. A 'good' doctor or practitioner is one who possesses the following qualities. Use the checklist when you visit a doctor, alternative practitioner or specialist.

- Is prepared to give you as much information as you ask for
- Outlines your choices of treatment and allows you to join in any decisions
- Is interested in encouraging you to help yourself
- Helps you to steer your way to the professionals who can help you, whether these are medical specialists or alternative practitioners
- Has empathy
- Has a positive outlook on life and knows how to look after him or herself as well as you
- Doesn't believe that he or she has the right answer to every problem
- Is a survivor

Now check out your side of the contract. Are you a 'good' patient? A 'good' patient is someone who:

- Is prepared to take responsibility for his or her illness
- Has a clear idea of what he or she expects from an appointment
- Is clear about the nature of the problem (the doctor will want to know how long you have had the symptoms, when

they occur, whether you've had the problem before, whether there are any associated symptoms such as changes in eating, bowel or sleeping habits)
- Presents symptoms as clearly and simply as possible and is honest about what is bothering him or her. Every doctor is familiar with the patient who waffles on about a series of trivial complaints, only to mention, as they are on their way through the door, 'Oh, by the way, doctor, there's this lump in my breast.' This may be a result of your own denial or fear
- Is prepared to ask honestly if he or she isn't satisfied with a diagnosis or explanation and expects an honest answer
- Recognises that he or she may need further tests and investigations and that even then it may not always be possible to come to a definitive diagnosis
- Is interested in his or her treatment. If the doctor prescribes drugs, ask exactly what they are supposed to do, how they should be taken, what side effects (if any) you might expect, and whether there are any foods, medicines or alcohol you should refrain from while you are on them. Don't forget to inform the doctor if you are allergic to any medication
- Doesn't expect the doctor to know everything and doesn't expect miracles

ILLNESS AND RELATIONSHIPS

Any illness affects your close relationships. All of us have a series of unwritten agreements with our partners. If something happens to disrupt these, for example if it's been assumed that you are very independent and energetic and then this changes through tiredness or illness, it can put your relationship under strain. Men, in particular, may have a problem with the feelings of weakness illness brings. They often feel they should be the protectors in a family, and experience a sense of failure when illness strikes.

- Be gentle with yourself and your partner, and recognise that it takes time to adjust to being ill
- Explain what you have found out about your condition to your partner but try not to let it dominate your life. Do things you enjoy together and forget about your illness from time to time
- Recognise that there are no right and wrong responses. The way your partner deals with your illness will be similar to the way he or she deals with other difficult situations. Don't expect your partner to react in the same way as you
- Recognise that every relationship has its ups and downs. Don't blow these out of proportion, and try to believe in your ability to pull through. Try to avoid minor irritants becoming major issues. Talk about them and try to be patient.

SURVIVING CHRONIC CONDITIONS OR ILLNESS

Although it is often a tremendous relief to know what is wrong with you, a diagnosis is just the beginning. Learning to live with the knowledge that you have a long-term condition can be immensely challenging. The discovery that you are suffering from a chronic illness is often an enormous blow to the self-confidence and the realisation that you may have to be on treatment and have regular check-ups for the rest of your life can be very difficult to cope with.

LIVING WITH LOSS

Illness is the loss of health. And just as with any kind of loss we experience grief. As well as the very real physical suffering, there is the loss of your self-image as a fit, healthy person. Our bodies, as you discovered in Chapter Two, reflect us and have a big effect on our self-confidence, a vital survivor quality. The physical effects of illness, accident or treatment such as disfigurement or hair loss, can be especially hard to bear, and can have a very real effect on our sense of identity. For example, women who have lost a breast in a mastectomy can feel their femininity is threatened. Drug treatment can lead to physical changes such as weight gain or loss. As Peter Speck says in his book *Loss, Grief and Medicine* (Balliere Tindall):

- *'If the body image is disrupted by . . . surgery, it can lead to a grief-like reaction, which requires a period of mourning before the resulting trauma is resolved and a new, acceptable, body-image is formed. The acceptance of this by others is important.'*

Treatment can often lead to other consequences too. For example, if you have had to have a hysterectomy and can no longer have children, you may feel a loss of status and purpose in life. You may feel as though it's your 'fault' if you and your partner had planned a family.

SURVIVING HOSPITAL

Medical diagnosis and treatment is frequently stressful, especially as it can take time to reach an accurate diagnosis. A hospital stay can be especially stressful as you have to be away from your own familiar surroundings and friends at a time when you are under stress. In a busy hospital clinic or ward, with so much going on, it's easy to feel lost, alone and isolated. Away from your own territory, and in the grip of an illness which is hard to understand, it is easy to feel powerless and depressed.

On the whole, smaller local units are usually friendlier, and you might want to consider them for routine, uncomplicated illnesses or conditions, such as a straightforward pregnancy. The larger, regional or teaching hospitals are usually better for severe, life-threatening or unusual conditions, or where treatment is complicated because you have more than one condition. Such hospitals are able to offer the most experienced specialists and the latest treatment. However, you may find the atmosphere less personal. Some hospitals, for example many cancer hospitals and units in the UK, now incorporate alternative and complementary therapies in their treatment programme. You may want to consider this when thinking about which hospital would be best for you.

Even in hospital, there is much you can do to help yourself. Finding out more about your illness can enable you to feel more in charge. However, if you prefer not to know too much about your illness, accept the way you are feeling and do what you feel is right for you. Some things you can do to help yourself include:

- Find out what your rights are in hospital. What are the visiting hours? Can you see your medical record? What are the rights regarding consent. In the UK you have to give your consent to all treatment. In the USA, the American Hospital Association issues Patients Bills of Rights. In the UK, you can get information from consumer groups such as The Patients Association
- Eat well. If hospital food leaves something to be desired, as it often does, ask visitors to bring in food and fruit
- Find out if there are any alternative therapies available in the hospital. If not, it may be possible to arrange for certain therapists to visit you
- Use relaxation, breathing and meditation (see Chapter Two) to help lift your mood and cope with the stress of being in hospital. Relaxation tapes are a good idea too
- Find a support person (see Chapter Four) to listen to your moans, help you think positively, and discuss things with the staff if you don't have the energy. Parents are now encouraged to stay with their children in hospital but sick adults need this sort of support too. Your ally can be your partner or a good friend, who is prepared to spend extra time with you. Try to arrange this beforehand so you know you have someone on whom you can rely to act as a go-between
- Bring in a few home comforts and reminders such as photos of your family, favourite postcards, a favourite blanket or rug, a plant, a personal tape or CD player, notepaper and so on

- Make sure you stay informed about your treatment. If there is anything you don't understand, don't be afraid to ask. Try to empathise with the staff and be assertive but not aggressive if you feel your needs are not being met

IF YOU NEED SURGERY

Part of being in control is being able to contribute to your treatment decisions. Not all operations are really necessary, so try to find out as much as you can about the operation that has been suggested beforehand and if you feel uncertain ask for a second opinion. Some questions to ask include:

- How long does the operation take?
- What are the possible complications?
- How many operations of this kind have you done?
- Will you personally do the operation?
- How long will it take me to recover?
- When can I go back to work?
- What can I do to aid recovery?

KEEPING UP YOUR CONFIDENCE

Illness can be a big blow to your self-confidence. You may feel unwilling to trust your body and that it has let you down. Accept that it takes time, but rest assured that, as your condition is brought under control and you begin to feel better, you will be able to deal with all the changes it has brought in your life and healing on a much wider level can take place. Many sufferers find that as they learn to live with a chronic or progressive condition they also learn new ways of thinking about their illness in the context of their lives. Remember that the Chinese word for 'crisis' means both 'danger' and 'opportunity'. If you can see your illness, however unwelcome, as opening up the prospect of positive growth and development, you will find it much easier to cope.

THINKING ABOUT YOUR ILLNESS

As with any major change, psychologists have discovered that thinking about a serious, chronic or progressive illness goes through several stages. At first, you feel numb, out of control and unable to act. Next comes minimisation, when you may describe your problem as something trivial or deny it altogether. This is often followed by a period of self-doubt and depression, as the reality sinks in. The low point in self-esteem is acceptance or letting go, when the reality of your illness hits home, and you begin to realise what it means to the way you lead your life.

However, as with so many changes, once you hit rock bottom, you begin to go up again, and your self-esteem begins to rise as you test your new situation, and begin to make positive changes in your life. Such changes can be something simple like joining an exercise class, or deciding to eat more healthily.

FINDING THE MEANING OF YOUR ILLNESS

It is usually no accident if your body breaks down or you are involved in an accident. If you have failed to be sensitive to your body's messages, becoming ill is your body's way of drawing attention to the fact that you need to take more rest, eat better, or that something is not right in your life. Learn to listen to your body and respect what it is trying to tell you. Sometimes, the reason for an illness or accident may be obvious. For example, if you have been driving yourself too hard at work and are then involved in a road accident because your mind was not fully on the road, the cause and effect is fairly obvious. However, sometimes the meaning is harder to disentangle. Psychologists have discovered that denied feelings about loss are often a factor in the development of illness. For example, men whose wives have died in the previous year are much more susceptible to developing cancer. Many sufferers from anorexia nervosa seem to have had a bereavement or be suffering from 'hidden guilt'. Suppressing your illness with drugs is not always a good idea, though of course if you are seriously ill and your body has broken down in a major way this may be necessary.

Even minor self-limiting illnesses such as coughs or colds can be signs that we need to take care of ourselves better. Louise Hay, whose self-help books have helped many people to find new meaning in their lives, suggests that it can be useful to ask yourself the following questions:

- Why have I developed this illness at this time?
- Who do I need to forgive?
- What is the truth that needs to be told?
- What is happening in my life at this time?
- Am I happy?
- What is my body telling me?
- What problem does this illness resolve?

According to Hay, 'the only thing we are ever dealing with is a thought, and thought can be changed'. Sounds familiar? It is the same idea we looked at in Chapter Five.

WHEN MIRACLES ARE POSSIBLE

All doctors are familiar with people who completely recover from serious illnesses with no apparent explanation. US physician Bernie Siegel, who wrote *Love, Medicine and Miracles*, has done much to increase our understanding of this phenomenon, which doctors describe as 'spontaneous remission'. What he found was that people who recovered, in other words survivors, were those who were able to listen to their bodies and find the meaning of their illness. He discovered that differences in the way we react to major illness can actually affect our chances of recovery.

Often, the message of your illness is that you need to regain your balance – remember that balance is an important part of the survivor personality. To do so, you may need to change the way you live, talk, think, feel, eat or spend your time. It's (relatively) easy to change the way you eat. It can be harder to accept that you need to change the way you feel. However, psychologists have found time and again that people who succumb to cancer are often those who usually suppress angry feelings, while people who are driven by anger are more likely to incur a heart attack. For one person, the message is to be less tolerant and forgiving and learn how to express anger, for the other, the message may be to become more tolerant and forgiving and be less angry.

As with all survival situations, there are no real rules: each person's way of becoming a survivor is different, so there is no 'how to' plan or formula. What worked for one person will not necessarily work for you, though it may inspire you to keep searching and experimenting to find your own answers. In fact the 'cure' for your illness is less in specific methods or treatment and more in taking responsibility for your recovery. For some people, it might mean using mental imagery or visualisation, for example one cancer patient imagined his white blood cells (the body's defensive cells) as huge white hunting dogs which could sniff out and destroy cancer cells, which he visualised as small rats.

FACING DEATH

Death is still one of the great taboos in our culture. However, as the great writer on death Elisabeth Kubler-Ross has written, 'We are all terminally ill. Once we recognise that, we enjoy the life we have left.' Dying is perhaps the biggest challenge any of us ever face, not only for the person who is dying but for those around them, including the professionals.

As with all changes, dying can be both an active and a passive process. It involves actively choosing as well as letting go. If you know that you are going to die you – and those around you – can prepare. Dying, like other challenges, involves going through a series of stages, which by now you are very familiar with. According to Elisabeth Kubler-Ross these are:

- Denial and isolation
  When faced with the news that they have a terminal illness, most people react with the thought 'No, not me. It can't be true.' According to Kubler-Ross, it's vital to accept and

respect this, 'We cannot look at the sun all the time, we cannot face death all the time. These patients can consider the possibility of their own death for a while but then have to put this consideration away in order to pursue life.'

- Anger
  At this stage, it is common to try and find someone or something to blame, and to have a wave of rage at having to curtail your plans and dreams for the future. If you are close to someone who is dying, take time to listen to the person.
- Bargaining
  This is the stage of 'If I do xxx, then I will get better.' You may attempt to bargain with yourself, the doctors or God. Sometimes the bargaining is a result of guilt and the feeling that you weren't 'good' enough to live.
- Depression
  When the reality sinks in, depression takes hold. People who are dying often go over their regrets at things left unachieved or unfinished. Focussing on what you have done and dealing with any unfinished business with the people around you can be tremendously liberating.
- Acceptance
  Finally, the person who is dying often starts to withdraw and no longer wants to be disturbed by the troubles of the rest of the world. At this stage, the person who is dying may prefer people simply to sit with them rather than talking.

TAKING CONTROL

When you are about to die it is still important to feel that you have choices and that your wishes will be respected. All the suggestions above about finding out about your illness and your options for care and treatment apply to terminal illness too. Even if staying in hospital or going into a hospice to die is the only real alternative, the person who is dying and those around them can have choices about what they want. Hospices are not intended to be just places where people go to die, they are places where they go to live the last days of their life. The boundaries between a hospice and home are not as strictly drawn as between a hospital and home. People are often encouraged to go home and their families to treat the hospice as their home.

Even at the very end of our lives, we can have control. Many people who are terminally ill hold out until a special event such as a wedding or the birth of a baby. Others choose to die. My ex-partner's 90-year-old grandmother told his father, 'I won't see you again' – even though she had walked through the village to see the family just that day and wasn't ill. She died that night.

FINDING THE GIFT

Finally, whatever the nature of your illness, survivors are those who are able to hold on to hope right until the end and find something positive to celebrate. One sufferer from thyroid disease told me:

- *Being ill has revealed to me a resilience I never knew I had, has taught me to value the good things in my life; my children, my friends. Now I take nothing for granted, no one at face value. I have gained a tiny insight into the even more serious illnesses that befall people and recognise their real courage in adversity. I begin to understand the isolation that can be felt by the differently abled in a torso-obsessed culture.'*

Another, who went through a period of depression, said:

- *'I always used to be rather impatient of people who were depressed, and think it was just a matter of them snapping out of it. When I experienced it myself, I realised it wasn't like that. I am now much more tolerant of friends who are depressed.'*

Even death can be a gift. The husband of a friend who recently died of cancer told me at her funeral:

- *'I am convinced that she didn't give up. I think she realised the only way to kill the cancer was to die. I believe she chose to die.'*

SURVIVING SICKNESS ROUNDUP

- I feel confident that I am able to listen to my body and understand its messages when my health breaks down
- I do not blame myself for my illness, but I accept responsibility for anything I may have done which has contributed to it and plan to do what I can to change
- I feel confident that I can find the information I need to deal with my illness
- I feel confident that I can find the right professionals (orthodox or alternative) to help me deal with my illness
- I feel confident that I can deal with the professionals
- I am ready to consider the possible course of my illness and plan what I can do to support myself whatever that might involve

Yes? Congratulations. On the other hand, if you didn't tick many of the boxes, don't worry. This hasn't been an easy chapter to write, and I'm sure it hasn't been an easy one to read. Use the insights you have gained to help you and return to them if you need to help you make changes and move on to the future – whatever that might be.

CHAPTER TEN
SURVIVING DISASTER

No-one likes to think about the worst things that could happen. However, as with all difficult experiences, when disaster strikes we cope better if we are able to make some sort of sense out of what has happened. This chapter is all about those times – losing a baby or child, being abused as a child or dealing with bereavement – when life reaches rock bottom, how to survive and start climbing back. For, though it is almost impossible to believe at the time, even life's most bruising experiences can offer you the chance to look at yourself afresh, broaden your perspective and find new meaning. The suggestions you will find in this chapter are not meant to be definitive instructions in how to deal with such major challenges. Rather, they are intended as a tentative map, which may help guide you as you reach inside yourself and find the resources you need to survive.

This chapter is all about how to survive some of life's worst losses. In it we look at how to cope with the death of a husband, wife, partner or close friend; how to cope with the loss of a baby or child, through miscarriage, abortion or stillbirth; and how to cope with being abused as a child, which results in a huge loss, that of your childhood – something you can never reclaim.

SURVIVING BEREAVEMENT

Grief is a natural reaction to loss and there aren't any right or wrong ways to go about it. Mourning is what we do when we grieve. Psychologists have described grieving as passing through a series of phases, that are very similar to the stages of change we have already looked at in some detail. However, as with change, seeing grief as a series of stages is just one way of understanding what is happening and trying to feel more in control of the seemingly chaotic and uncontrollable thoughts, emotions and feelings we may be experiencing.

Each bereavement has things in common and yet each is different. The way we grieve and our experience of grief are different for each of us too. It is affected by the way the person or thing we have lost died, our previous experience of loss and how we have dealt with it, and what the person or thing we have lost meant to us. For this reason, some psychologists, who have studied death and bereavement, prefer to visualise grief as a whirlpool in which our emotions spin wildly out of control. The water in the whirlpool (our emotions) may dash against rocks, giving rise to pain and physical symptoms, or it may wash up on the shore and remain stuck in pools. Eventually, however, it flows through the period of mourning as we come to accept the loss we have sustained and rejoin the river of life.

SURVIVING THE DEATH OF YOUR PARTNER

The death of a partner or close friend is, quite literally, one of the most serious threats to survival. Research shows that the chances of dying yourself soar in the first six months after losing a husband, wife or partner. The way your partner died, the circumstances in which he or she died, the age of your partner at their death, and many other factors will affect the way you think about his or her death. And, as always, the way you think about what happens is crucial. The emotional wounds following an accidental or sudden death, or the death of a younger adult, for example, can be especially hard to close; because it seems so unfair, it is often difficult to make sense of his or her death. Likewise, if you were so close as a couple that you built your world entirely around your partner, it is also often harder to come to terms with. You may have let other friendships drop or find it hard to 'connect' with other people and draw sustenance from their support.

Accepting and expressing your emotions, as discussed in Chapter Three, is vital to survival. No one can shorten your grief or stop the pain. However, the more you allow yourself to feel, the easier it will be to celebrate your partner's life and to experience the joy as well as the pain that comes from death.

SURVIVING THE LOSS OF A BABY OR CHILD

Our children are our hope for the future. For this reason the death of a baby or child is one of the most devastating experiences anyone can have. Miscarriage, termination, stillbirth, cot death or accidental death are especially hard losses to bear, because they threaten to stifle hope, our belief in the future. Such deaths turn life's natural order upside down. It can be hard to avoid feeling overwhelmed and isolated by a grief that brings with it not just the usual feelings, but also involves having to find a way to come to terms with the idea that while you have the rest of your life before you, your child has not.

It is cold comfort to be told that one in five pregnancies ends in a miscarriage or that 20 babies a day are stillborn or die shortly after birth if it happens to you. The way you react to your loss will be unique to you and your partner. However, there are certain common themes. In the case of stillbirth and miscarriage, other people don't always recognise that the baby who died was just as much a real person as an older child. Because your loss may be 'invisible' (if you were in the early days of pregnancy, you may not even have told other people you were pregnant) it can be easy to get trapped in the early stage of denying or hiding your grief. Talking to other people who have also lost a baby in this way, or contacting a self-help group such as the Miscarriage

Association, or SANDS (Stillbirth and Neonatal Death Society), whose members have all undergone these painful experiences themselves, can help.

If the baby died before birth, it can be especially painful and poignant to give birth to a dead baby and to see other parents celebrating their joy at a new arrival when all you have is an empty cradle. After stillbirth or late miscarriage, the cruel physical reminders – bleeding, breast tenderness, and the production of milk – are painful evidence of your loss and can add to the misery and guilt you may be feeling. You may feel guilty and blame yourself, fearing that something you did – or didn't do – was responsible for your baby's death.

GUIDELINES FOR GRIEVING

The following guidelines may help you to make sense of your loss. They aren't rules, simply things that many people who have experienced bereavement find helpful.

- Accept your emotions
  Accept your emotions and allow yourself to grieve in the way that feels right for you. Grief can involve certain recognisable phases – disbelief, denial, yearning, anger, guilt, depression, anxiety and acceptance. However, don't feel that you have to go through these in order to grieve properly. Try not to force yourself to react in a particular way or blame yourself if you don't. Allow the different emotions to come and go.
- Expect your emotions to vary in intensity
  You may be surprised by how your moods swing from day to day. Accept that your emotions may be conflicting and don't try to change them. Accept that you will have good days and bad days. If you have lost a baby even though you are full of sadness you may at first have moments of the euphoria that almost all of us feel after birth. If you have worries that something you did could

have caused your baby's death, talk over your fears with a doctor or nurse.

- **Accept that there is a purpose to your emotions**
You may have a deep desire to know exactly why the person you have lost died. You may find yourself physically searching and listening for the person you have lost. You may even imagine that you see him or her, only to realise that it was someone else. This is your mind's way of coming to terms with your loss. Give yourself time and recognise that your search for reasons is a part of trying to make sense of what has happened. Remind yourself that there is a purpose behind your feelings. You are entitled to feel them, to talk about them and to express them. Cry if you feel like it and don't be afraid to share your misery with those who are close to you. If you don't feel like crying, however, don't force yourself.

- **Keep some reminders**
Painful though they may be at first, having a tangible reminder of the person you have lost makes it easier to grieve. Don't rush to get rid of that person's belongings, however difficult it may be to see them. If you have lost an older person or child, you will have plenty of keepsakes; if you experienced a miscarriage, termination or stillbirth, you will have fewer. Naming your baby can help you visualise him or her more easily and enable you to talk more easily about him or her. Keep and look at other reminders of your baby, for example his/her birth certificate, a lock of hair, a print-out of your baby's heart rate, a photo of your baby and/or of an ultrasound scan, the plastic bracelet that was put around his/her wrist at birth, or cards sent by friends. Writing an account of your baby's birth or of what he or she looked like may help some people.

- **Celebrate the person's life**
A ritual such as a funeral, religious ceremony or other gathering to celebrate the life of the person you have lost

and mourn his or her death is an important part of grieving. It gives you the opportunity to express your feelings with others who care for you. And though it may be an ordeal, such a get-together often has a positive side. You will probably be warmed by other people's love and support. Arranging such a ceremony for a baby is very important. Organisations such as SANDS and The Miscarriage Association can help you.

CHILDHOOD LESSONS

Tragically, for some people, childhood is a harrowing time of abuse and betrayal. One study of sexual abuse found that in the UK, 27% of men and 59% of women had been sexually abused as children, using a broad definition of abuse that included flashing, being touched, being pressured to have sex as well as actual assaults and rapes. Other studies using a narrower definition put the figures at 8% of men and 12% of women.

Adult survivors of sexual abuse often experience feelings of shame, guilt, depression, low self-image, self-blame, disgust, anger, hate, love and confusion. Victims may attempt to ease the pain by abusing drugs, alcohol, food, sex or developing chronic pelvic pain. But not all children who have been abused have such reactions. Many display amazing resilience in the face of horrific experiences. How? The secret seems to be finding the hidden gift in adversity, the thing that enables you to keep going and come through stronger and wiser. One survivor I spoke to said,

- *'It was having the love of my grandmother. Even though she was the mother of the person who abused me – my uncle – she always believed in me completely. I think that gave me the confidence to realise I was a worthwhile person and to survive.'*

DEALING WITH YOUR EMOTIONS

As with any crisis, the survivor sequence starts with handling your emotions. Accepting what happened, owning your emotions and dealing with guilt, one of the most prevalent emotions in abuse victims, can be a first step on the long road to healing. A psychiatric nurse describing how she began to rebuild her life writes in the UK journal *Nursing Times*:

- *'Memories of that abuse which I carried around I pushed deep inside, afraid that if they came out I would be ostracised, lose my friends and my job. But worse still was the fear that if I acknowledged what happened I would again be engulfed by the feelings I had tried to suppress. Who wants to be the daughter of a sex abuser? It was hard for me to acknowledge that I was a victim of abuse, as I always believed I initiated a relationship with my dad, that I had asked for sex, wanted it . . . I could not comprehend that by working through so much trauma I might actually become free from an invisible threat that I felt bound me so tightly.'*

She describes how she had coped by blocking off her emotions and her resentment at being forced to relive her painful memories:

- *'I felt numb, except for a pain in my chest that would not go away. I could not even get angry; it was nobody's fault that my dad was sick, he loved me so . . . My mind and feelings had been separated for so long.'*

It's important to take your time and not expect too much too soon. Power and powerlessness are often big issues for survivors and it is vital to feel able to make your own decisions and take control of what happens in your life. It's important to recognise that you are a normal, healthy individual who has responded in your own way to a serious life crisis.

- Recognise that at the time you made the choices you had to At the time the abuse happened, faced with the prospect of losing your family and those you loved, you may have

chosen to go along with the abuse. But that doesn't make what happened your fault. Learn to believe that you are now in charge of your life.
- Hold on to your desire to be different
  Another feature identified by the experts as vital for resilience is the desire to be different. In the *Nursing Times* article, the author writes:

- *'I was encouraged to work on the relationship with my daughter. I began to lose that fear that I was the image of my own mother whom I hated so much.'*

- Talk to others who have been through similar experiences
  Many abuse survivors find it helpful to join a self-help group for survivors where they can share experiences, break down isolation and loneliness, explore different perspectives on their problems, find friends and gain the sense of control that is often the first step in change. Research by Rosalyn Barber, herself a survivor of childhood sexual abuse, suggests that one of the main benefits is being accepted and heard. One of the women who took part in her research attended the group for a year before she felt able to speak,

- *'Before that I used to be curled up in the corner of a chair with my back to everyone and my hair all over my face so they couldn't see me. And I would just rock backwards and forwards the whole time . . . it was brilliant that the group allowed me to do that – no one judged you or thought you were . . . a nutcase. It was just the acceptance . . . everyone belongs.'*

- Find a therapist
  Talking to a professional therapist can help, if you can find someone you can trust. Many survivors prefer a therapist who is also a survivor.
- Accept your emotions and recognise that they will pass
  As we saw in Part One, your emotions are neither good nor bad – they simply are. Learning to believe this, to express

your emotions and let them go, can be tremendously healing.
- Challenge 'automatic' thoughts
  Cognitive therapy in which you are encouraged to stop your thought process and challenge distorted beliefs can also be very effective. You may need to confront the myths surrounding rape and abuse that somehow women or girls attract violence and enjoy rape.
- Find the gift
  The final stage in the survivor sequence, and in healing, is always to find the gift. The nurse mentioned earlier sums this up when she writes:
- *'The outside world is looking different to me now. Once it was me against the world, now I see thousands of people chasing their dreams and their fantasies, some good, some bad. All those mental mechanisms aiding avoidance make me want to say "Stop and turn around, you might be amazed at what you find."'*

LISTENING AND LEARNING

LISTENING TO SURVIVORS

If someone you know or are involved with has survived a distressing experience you may be called upon to listen to them. Doing so involves special listening skills. Be aware of your own strengths and weaknesses. If you don't feel up to it, don't be afraid to suggest that you help the survivor to find a professional counsellor or therapist or seek out a support group.

- **Don't ask the person about their experiences unless you can handle honest answers**
  Bear in mind that listening to someone who has survived life's worst horrors demands great emotional strength. Avoid asking someone to tell you about very distressing

experiences at times when you are feeling in need of a lot of emotional support yourself.

- **Be prepared to hear the person out once they have opened up**

    Provided you are feeling reasonably robust emotionally, you should be able at least to listen to what the other person has lived through. Survivors of major, distressing experiences will usually talk to someone who has the courage to listen.

- **Give the person plenty of time**

    It is often difficult for survivors of deeply painful experiences to find someone who can listen to their full story. If you ask, be prepared to listen for hours. It's vital to allow the person who has suffered plenty of time to talk and not to interrupt to share your own feelings and opinions.

- **Be an active listener**

    People who have survived an unhappy or brutal childhood were often forced to put on the 'happy family' act in public. Even years later it can be difficult to drop that front. You can encourage them and get a better picture of what they had to endure by putting into practice the skills of active listening. If you feel puzzled about facts or incidents, ask for clarification. Remember the stages of change and try to get some idea of the time scale of events by talking the person through from beginning to end. Ask for details. Find out what happened, what it was like for them and how they felt at each stage.

- **Don't force the person to be negative about the situation**

    Remember the important rule of survival: it's not what happens but how you react to it that counts. Resist the temptation to tell the person you are talking to what it was like for them. Accept their version of events. Do not insist on what a horrific experience it was if they didn't see it that way. That is your version of the truth. It isn't necessarily theirs. Survivors often find that they encounter people who have a deep need to help others. Such people have a script which is based on rescuing others. Such a script involves the survivor taking on a victim role. Survivors often remain silent when forced to be with people who need them to feel bad or victimised. It's vital to be an honest listener and to be open to the way in which the person reacted, not how you would react.

- **Listen with compassion but minimise sympathy**
  It's easier for people to talk about the most painful parts of an experience if you are matter of fact but calm. Expressions of sympathy like, 'Poor you!' and 'How awful!' can prevent people from fully opening up. Control your imagination and resist taking on the other person's emotions. Don't force the survivor to handle your emotions as well as his or her own. If you need emotional support, get it elsewhere. If the person relives moments of distress, accept their feelings and don't tell them they mustn't have them. Stay with them.

- **Find out what the survivor has found that is positive in the experience**
  Remember 'the gift' to be found in unhappy experiences. Not all people who have gone through pain are scarred for life. In fact, many become more mature, rounded human beings as a result of their bad experiences. And, of course, that is what this book is all about. Listening to survivors talk will enable you to discover for yourself how the same circumstances that are traumatic for some people can cause others to become stronger. Ask if they believe one thing kept them going and contributed to their survival more than anything else.

- **Reflect on what you have discovered**
  Think about what the person has told you and what it means to you. Use their experience to ask new questions – and discover new answers – about resilience, survival and thriving.

LEARNING FROM SURVIVORS

Can we learn anything from people who have survived experiences such as being taken hostage, torture, prison camps and others of the worst conditions human beings can endure? Yes. Such extreme circumstances call for extreme survival measures. Survivors in such situations cannot afford the luxury of emotions. It is not usually safe to express their anger, rage and distress so they have to contain them. Survivors possess a fierce will to stay alive, what one prison camp survivor has described as 'a life force from within'. Even in situations of extreme hardship, survivors are able to develop empathy for others, such as their guards or captors, which allow them to develop a more human relationship with them. They learn to 'love their enemy' and in return may receive small acts of kindness. Some survivors project themselves into their future. This gives them hope which enables them to rise above their suffering. Others escape into vivid fantasies, or visualisations. Almost all learn to tap into the worlds of sights, sounds and smells. Even in the most extreme of circumstances the sound of a bird singing can bring a moment of joy. Another characteristic is the ability of such survivors to resist, to test and break the rules in some small way. Finally, even in the most desperate circumstances, survivors are able to maintain a strong sense of humour. The lessons of such survivors are ones we can all learn from. Survivors never forget their memories, but once they have escaped they are able to integrate their experiences and stay alive.

FINDING THE GIFT

Auschwitz survivor, Eva Eger, says:

- *'You must be strong to forgive. Forgiveness is not condoning or excusing. Forgiveness has nothing to do with justice. Forgiving is a selfish act to free yourself from being controlled by your past.'*

Her words contain a lesson for all survivors. Your past experiences will always be a part of you. You can't rub them out, however much you would like to do so. However, even the most painful experiences can be dealt with so that they don't ruin your life. It is also possible that, by working to overcome your emotional trauma, you can go beyond recovery and reach a higher, better, stronger version of yourself than you ever imagined existed.

SURVIVING DISASTER ROUNDUP

Like the last chapter, this has been a difficult one to write and, I am sure, to read. Having read it, however, perhaps you feel stronger and more able to deal with the losses you have experienced in your life or may face in the future.

- I am able to accept my losses without dwelling on them unduly or ignoring them
- I understand the importance of accepting my feelings, whatever they are, in the face of loss
- I feel confident that I can deal with future losses
- I feel able to listen to people who have suffered unhappy experiences
- I feel confident I can help them to find the help they need if I cannot listen myself
- I feel able to look for 'the gift' in any loss I may experience

If you were a victim of child abuse:

- I can appreciate the good and bad aspects of my childhood
- I do not blame myself for what happened

If you have ticked all, or most, of the above, then you are well on your way to recovery – and survival.

CHAPTER ELEVEN
SURVIVING YOUR FUTURE

The Survivor Personality has, I hope, given you some ideas about how to develop the resilience you need to survive life. Once you have worked on developing your own resilience you can call on it whenever you need to, for the rest of your life. As well as all the strategies we have looked at in previous chapters, there are plenty of other ways you can add to your capacity for survival in the weeks, months and years ahead. This chapter is about surviving your future. It is intended to tie up some of the themes we have looked at throughout the book, introduce some new ones and help you focus on some more ways in which you can develop your survivor qualities from now on.

FUTURE SHOCK

You may remember from Part One the importance to survival of having a full life. Having a full life doesn't just apply to the things you do; it also applies to how you think and who you are. Survivors survive by being rounded people. In the past, survival depended on learning who you were as a child and sticking to it for the rest of your life. Our parents and grandparents pinned their identity on their ethnic group, their religion, their jobs, their gender or their personality. Secure they were certainly, but the price to be paid for such security could be a heavy one. For, as we've seen in this book, sticking rigidly to the labels you have pinned on yourself can hinder your ability to survive.

In today's rapidly changing world, flexibility is the name of the game. Let's just take one example from the sex war. The phrase 'Real men don't eat quiche' has become something of a joke. Even so, the fact remains that efforts to be a 'real man' or 'real woman' are only successful when we find someone who is able to play the complementary part. The trouble is that in such rigid partnerships, problems are virtually guaranteed if something happens to disturb the equilibrium. If the man loses his job, the woman loses respect for him because he is no longer the 'breadwinner.' If the woman rises higher in her career, the man may accuse her of usurping his territory. Imposing such restrictions on ourselves locks us into a frustrating and limited existence.

The survivor way, by contrast, opens us up to new ways of being. The most important question when a baby is born becomes not, 'Is it a boy or a girl?' (in any case the advent of ultrasound and other windows on the womb often makes such a question superfluous), but 'Is it healthy?' A healthy individual is one who is encouraged to develop their own personality and encouraged to explore their own interests and individuality. In today's world, the way to survive is to be both trusting *and* cautious, selfish *and* unselfish, tough *and* loving, intuitive *and* logical . . . and so on.

BRINGING UP A SURVIVOR

Anyone who has had children knows that bringing them up is one of the most difficult and challenging tasks any of us face, but it can also be exciting and rewarding. If you have children, you are able to help another human being (your child) to develop the ability to survive. The importance of the way we bring up our children is underlined in everything from newspaper accounts of crime rates to the stories we read in the gossip columns of 'Hollywood children', the offspring of celebrities who, for all their material advantages, often end up as non-survivors. Use the suggestions over the next few pages to spark off some ideas about how you can help your child develop into a survivor. However, do bear in mind that as a parent you can only do your best for your children. None of us ever gets it completely right – and human beings would probably be a lot more dull and boring if we did! If you try to be responsive to each child's individual needs, you can't go far wrong.

WHAT'S LOVE GOT TO DO WITH IT?

As we've seen, love is the biggest key to survival. But – and it's back to the power of feelings here – it's not enough just to love your children; you must also express your love by cuddling and hugging them, celebrating their successes, helping them to come to terms with their failures, showing interest in their doings (yes, even if you aren't particularly interested in roller-blading), and finding ways to tell them you love them. It's also important that you respect your children as individuals and love them unconditionally for who they are, not who you want or think they should be.

RESPECTING YOUR CHILDREN'S DIFFERENCES

Even as babies some children seem to be easier going than others. There may be all sorts of reasons for this, for example a difficult birth, basic temperament and so on, but it's important as a parent to cater for your children individually and not to discriminate against them even if they are very different from you. As parents we may find it easier to get on with one of our children than another, just as we find it easier to get on with some adults more than others. Some of this can be to do with your own personality; if you are the life and soul of the party, you may find it harder to understand a child who has a tendency to be shy. Even so, it's important for survival to take into account individual differences and to respect each of your children's needs. A child who is shy and clinging needs you to provide plenty of opportunities to explore the world, safe in the knowledge that you are there; a quiet child may need to spend more time with you; a boisterous child needs plenty of opportunities to let off steam and so on. You may need to give special time and attention to understanding a child who is very different from you. And it can also be a good idea to provide opportunities for him or her to spend time with, for example, a friend or relative who shares his or her interests and skills. Avoid pinning labels like 'good-natured' or 'clumsy' on your children. Avoid showing favouritism and never make one of your children a scapegoat in family rows or when things go wrong.

SPREADING THE LOVE AROUND

Another factor in helping your children to grow up as survivors is to encourage them to develop loving relationships with a wider range of different people. It was the father of psychology, Sigmund Freud, who first discovered the importance of the mother/child relationship in the early days of this century. Freud's ideas were sometimes misinterpreted by popular culture – Alfred Hitchcock's film *Psycho* is good example of the myth that a child with an unhealthy relationship with his mother could grow up psychopathic.

The next major discoveries about the way in which babies become attached to the people who look after them were made back in 1969 by the British psychiatrist John Bowlby, who found that babies – and their parents – were biologically programmed to bond with each other. Unfortunately, Bowlby's theories, coming at a time when women were returning to the kitchen, led to the idea that a mother's place was in the home and that children would be irreversibly damaged if their mothers went out to work.

The latest research suggests that the key factor is actually being able to form strong ties with people who care for you and respond to your needs. Those people can be your mother, father, granny, nanny or childminder, and it doesn't matter if it's one person or several so long as they love and care for you.

Sharing the caring as parents and encouraging your children to have good relationships with other people such as grandparents, the parents of other children and other grown-ups, can be a key factor in helping them to withstand life's stresses. For instance, research into children who have a mother or father who is mentally ill has revealed that children who have a strong relationship with the other parent, a relative or someone outside the family, tend to be more resilient.

YOU NEED FRIENDS

Like all of us, children also need friends of their own age. Intriguingly, in recent years the experts have discovered that having strong friendships during childhood and the teenage years is even more important for growing into a secure, happy adult than the parent/child relationship during babyhood. Incredibly, even babies as young as a year old become attached to each other and will seek out their special friend at toddler group, have loud babbling 'conversations' with each other and search for each other when one is missing. The importance of having good friends can't be over-emphasised in difficult times, as we've seen time and again. You can help your children develop friendship skills from an early age by providing them with the opportunities to meet and mix with other children. When they have to undergo difficult experiences, for example divorce or bereavement, you can encourage your children to gain strength by talking to others who have gone through similar things.

BREEDING SELF-CONFIDENCE

As you'll know from reading the rest of the book, self-esteem and self-confidence are important facets of the survivor personality. From an early age you can help to foster your children's confidence by showing that you love them just as they are, and by encouraging them to succeed in the things they do. It's not difficult to do but it does mean being sensitive to your child's changing needs and interests at different ages. Success helps breed self-confidence. So learn to notice what your child enjoys doing and does well and give him or her plenty of opportunities to develop his or her skills in those areas.

As we've already seen, one of the arts of survival is the ability to make plans and to feel that you are in control of your own life. The British psychiatrist Michael Rutter discovered that children who believed they were in control and made plans to shape their lives were more resilient than those who felt they were at the mercy of fate.

You can help your children develop planning skills by encouraging them to see cause and effect. Even small babies are able to appreciate cause and effect, and as your child grows older you can help him or her to see the connections between one thing and another by showing them, pointing them out and being prepared to answer their seemingly endless 'Why?s' with a patient explanation.

You can also help your child to develop another vital survival skill, empathy, the ability to tune into other people's feelings. For example, a small child can be helped to understand why his sister is so upset when he snatches one of her toys. Older children can be encouraged to discuss things that have happened to them and the way they and other people reacted. As your children get older you can encourage them to set goals, develop plans and put them into action, pacing yourself to them and allowing them to develop their independence gradually.

· FOSTERING RESILIENCE

As we've already seen, resilience develops not by protecting children from difficult experiences but by helping them to deal with them. Challenges and difficulties are a necessary part of growing up and children need to learn how to cope with them. You can help your children by giving them a range of different experiences in which they can test their skills, bearing in mind their age and stage of development. Research has shown, for example, that children cope better with a negative separation, such as going into hospital or a parent going into hospital, if they have previously had opportunities to experience 'happy separation'. So make sure your child has plenty of experiences such as going to play with friends, staying at playgroup or nursery, spending the night at a friend's house or going to stay with grandparents.

You can help your children to approach potentially stressful situations and experiences in a positive frame of mind, with the confidence that they can deal with the situation. Honesty is important, so children learn to acknowledge if they have been hurt mentally or physically. For instance, if your child has to have an operation, be honest about the fact that he or she is likely to feel sore afterwards, but point out the benefits too, for example it will enable him or her to be more active and play with other children or whatever. Above all, resilience comes from accepting your children for who they are and encouraging them to be themselves with their own unique ways of seeing, feeling, thinking and doing.

BECOMING A SURVIVOR AT WORK, REST AND PLAY

Bringing up our children in the ways suggested will help them to develop the skills and attributes they need to survive adult life. As adults, as we've seen survival depends on having a full life and developing a rounded personality.

THE SURVIVOR AT WORK

Work, as we've seen in Chapter Eight, is important because it provides opportunities for success, for friendship with others, and for increasing self-esteem. Today it's increasingly recognised — both by employers and workers — that the way to survive is to be flexible.

At work, a survivor is:

- Able to ask questions and listen well
- Quick to grasp what other people are feeling
- Able to admit when he or she doesn't know something
- In possession of all-round skills in dealing with people, tasks and relationships
- Not thrown by bad news and calm in emergencies
- Ready to give time to other people, but doesn't let people waste his or her time
- Self-confident and optimistic and creates a positive atmosphere
- Capable of making tough decisions when required
- Able to get jobs done in several different ways
- Able to explain what he or she is doing, how and why
- Capable of doing unpleasant parts of the job (such as giving someone the sack)
- Up-to-date in his or her field of work and with any new technology and always seeking to learn
- Able to acknowledge and thank other people for their efforts
- Someone with their own personal style
- Able to monitor results, welcome feedback and criticism, and take responsibility for mistakes
- Able to have other interests outside the job

THE SURVIVOR IN RELATIONSHIPS

Satisfying personal relationships – love again – are another key factor in survival. Indeed, research into resilience has revealed that having a happy marriage or relationship helps strengthen the resilience of people who have suffered unhappy or difficult childhoods. You'll find hints on how to find the partner who fits your needs in the companion to this book, *How To Get What You Want*. In the meantime, let's look at some of the characteristics of the survivor personality in personal relationships.

> In relationships, survivors are people who:
>
> - Feel confident enough to respect their partner and allow them the space to be themselves
>
> - Know how to express their love, appreciation and commitment to their partner and find ways to do so often
>
> - Are able to ask their partner for what they need without bullying or manipulating
>
> - Have defined clearly what each partner expects with regard to important issues such as fidelity, having children, money and come to some agreement
>
> - Accept that intimate relationships involve give and take and are prepared to work at this
>
> - Are prepared to be open and share their feelings – both good and bad – with their partner
>
> - Take responsibility for ensuring that their sex lives are as good as they can be
>
> - Are prepared to air differences with their partner without feeling that this threatens the end of the relationship

- Aren't tied to rigid male/female roles within their relationship (i.e. allow the male partner to develop and express his softer, more feeling side and the female partner to develop and express 'masculine' qualities such as assertiveness)

THE SURVIVOR AND FRIENDSHIP

Our jobs, lovers and partners may come and go. Our children grow up and no longer need us in the way they did when they were smaller. However, our friends often last a lifetime. Our friends can give us a sense of stability and a feeling of belonging in a world that rarely stays still. They are there to lean on in times of difficulty and are there to share in the fun and celebrate the good times. Friendships don't just happen. Survivors recognise the importance of strong friendships and are prepared to work at them, not in any heavy, laboured way but in a spirit of fun, mutual support and sharing.

In friendships, the survivor:

- Knows what kind of friendships he or she needs
- Is able to decide how much time and effort they have to put into friendships
- Takes the opportunity to make new friends in all kinds of different situations (work, leisure activities, charity work)
- Has more than one friend and doesn't expect every friend to supply everything he or she needs
- Values his or her friends as individuals and feels comfortable with their differences
- Is able to describe, negotiate and ask for what he or she wants from the friendship and reciprocate

- Is able to compromise when necessary
- Is not in competition with his or her friends
- Is able to talk about the friendship in a non-threatening way
- Is able to enjoy different activities with different friends
- Is able to refuse to give help to a friend when it demands more than he or she is able to give at that time, yet still be supportive
- Is able to accept without resentment that certain friends may not have the resources to give help whenever he or she needs it
- Is able to cut free from friendships that have ceased to be mutually sharing or nurturing
- Is able to have fun with friends

SURVIVING BEING A SURVIVOR

Now you have become a survivor, don't expect life to be plain-sailing from now on. Being a survivor can be tough at times. You may find yourself in situations where you have to stand up for what you believe in rather than what other people find they are comfortable with. There may be many times you have to swim against the tide and risk misunderstanding or criticism. On such occasions you will need all your courage and belief in yourself to enable you to survive. As always, knowing what you are up against enables you to arm yourself. Here is a list of some of the challenges you may face now you have become a survivor:

- Learning about yourself isn't always fun
  Your growing ability to tune into your own and other people's thoughts and emotions can be uncomfortable,

even painful, at times. You may discover things you don't like about yourself. There may be times when you become aware of hypocrisy, faults and defects in yourself: after all, no one is perfect, least of all survivors. There may be other times when you feel stupid and remorseful at something you have done.

ACTION! Make learning in life your number one goal and make the most of your discoveries and insights into the way you tick.

- You may confuse people

Some people may misunderstand your ability to be flexible. People who think in black and white terms will not be able to appreciate the way you see both sides of a question or your ability to change your way of thinking about something. If you don't keep quiet, people who have a rigid perspective may label you as 'negative', a trouble-maker or a poor team player.

ACTION! Make your intentions clear to those around you. Always explain what you think and what you intend to do about situations.

- You risk being an outcast

Group dynamics are such that if you dare to voice an opposing opinion you risk being rejected. The groups you are involved with at work, rest and play may find it hard to appreciate that you can understand 'the opposition' without necessarily agreeing with it. At the same time, in face-to-face encounters with the opposition, you may find it hard to get across that you can understand the way they look at things while not agreeing with their solution.

ACTION! Make it clear that just because you understand opposing viewpoints doesn't mean you agree with them.

- You never feel 'grown up'

Doing things in new ways, thinking new thoughts, having new feelings can be exciting, but it's not always easy. You can expect to make mistakes and feel unsure of yourself during times of transition or turning points. As a result you may never feel quite 'finished' or grown up.

ACTION! Realise that changing involves risks. Find the support you need and believe in yourself.

- 'Your way' may not be accepted

When you explain to people how you survived and what you did, instead of gaining acceptance and congratulation, you may find other people chipping in with, 'What I would have done is . . .

ACTION! Hold on to your sense of humour.

- Your advice can backfire

The solutions to the problems that people bring to you may seem obvious. It can be hard to accept that many people don't want answers when they complain about something, they just want an audience. Offering practical suggestions can strain the relationship.

ACTION! Know when to bide your time and when to offer advice.

- You may arouse jealousy

People who succeed in making things happen for themselves can become the butt of envy on the part of others. Your success may be dismissed as luck, and you may have to brace yourself for jibes from those who believe that because what you have done looks easy – it was.

ACTION! Accept them as part of a noisy planet and give yourself a pat on the back.

- You are always expected to be strong

Because you have overcome adversity, other people may be unwilling to allow you to have moments of weakness. They won't allow you to lean on them – even when you ask for their help – and refuse to give you the nurturing and support they take for granted from you.

ACTION! At times when you need support don't be afraid to ask for help from people close to you. Tell other people about your needs and learn to express them.

- You may not always be liked
  You may have to get tough from time to time to make things work. There may be occasions when you refuse to help someone who you can see is creating his or her own problems. You may need to let that person struggle, or hold back and let others see the results of their actions.

  ACTION! Realise that tough love is sometimes necessary and bear in mind that you don't have to be liked by everybody to be a worthwhile person.

- You don't know when to give up
  By being so determined to reach your goals you may never give up, even when it would be the best course to do so.

  ACTION! Make it part of your survival strategy to monitor your efforts to succeed and ask yourself from time to time, 'What would happen if I let this go?' (For more hints on pursuing goals see *How To Get What You Want*).

- You may be too sensitive
  Developing the ability to pick up other people's thoughts and feelings can expose you to their distress and pain. At times, you may find it hard to distinguish between their fears and distress and your own feelings. Confronted with someone who is sending out messages of anger, for example, you may become angry yourself. You may then find it difficult to act because you are unsure what you are feeling.

  ACTION! Give yourself time to track the origin of emotions you are feeling and refuse to 'own' those which don't belong to you.

- You may be criticised for taking care of yourself
  If you attempt to extricate yourself from a situation or relationship in which your energies are being drained, those involved may attempt to hook you back in by becoming even more extreme and manipulative in their behaviour. They may blame you for their distress, and

because you are able to tune into their feelings you will see their point of view. For example, the partner of a woman who attempts to leave an abusive relationship may become even more violent or abusive in an attempt to get her to stay. She, in turn, may feel sorry for him.

ACTION! Bear in mind that their insensitivity to you and their refusal to take equal responsibility for handling the difficulties you face is one reason why you are pulling away.

- You may become unpopular

Blowing the whistle on things that you perceive to be wrong doesn't always go down well. Instead of being thanked for your pains you may be told not to rock the boat and, if you still refuse to be silenced, seen as disloyal or not 'a team player'. Even worse, if your conscience obliges you to go public about an injustice, there may be attempts to smear your reputation and discredit you.

ACTION! Provide for your own safety by taking legal or other advice.

LEARNING WHAT CAN'T BE TAUGHT

Now we have come to the end of *The Survivor Personality*, it's time to face up to a contradiction: no one can teach you how to have a survivor personality! The more you allow someone who doesn't know you – whether that is a teacher, trainer or me, the writer you have never met – to shape you into becoming a more ideal person, the less chance you have of developing your own survivor style.

Bear in mind that this book, as with everything else that has been written about survival, resilience, hardiness, thriving, coping and positive thinking, describes a point of view. True, it contains the results of research together with some of the things I have learnt from my own experience and from other people I have met and talked to. However, remember that what you may be confronted with in your future, and your unique combination of strengths and capabilities, are yours and yours alone. Only you can learn to survive. Survival often, perhaps always, depends on how well you understand your reality, and the steps you take to make it work – for you.

What you can do is to devise your own plan for dealing with change, crisis and the unexpected. You may want to include some of the following:

- Ask questions
  Stay curious and interested in what is going on around you. When change, new developments, threats, confusion, trouble and criticism come your way learn to ask, 'What is happening here?'

- Increase your flexibility of thought and feeling
  Tell yourself that there is nothing wrong with feeling and thinking in both one way and its opposite. Free yourself from those inner messages which may be telling you that you 'must', 'should' or 'ought to' think or feel in a certain way. Develop many ways of responding to choices.

- Assume that change and uncertainty are certain
  Change, ambiguity and the unknown are a way of life in today's world. Learn to handle them with assurance and self-confidence. Increase your skills in turning new developments to your advantage.

- Develop your ability to tune into other people – especially people you find difficult
  Put yourself in other people's place. Ask, 'Why do they feel and think as they do? What are their views, assumptions, explanations and needs? How do they gain from acting as they do?' Govern your own actions not by what you intend but by the actual effect you have on others.

- Learn to value your own contribution
  In any situation ask yourself, 'What can I do so as to make things better for everyone?' Your ability to find ways to be useful increases your value. In every situation make it a habit to make your contribution more valuable than anyone thought it would be. By so doing you are investing in yourself.

- Learn how to learn from experience
  In this way you are always becoming more capable. Practise thanking those who tell you unpleasant things about yourself. Remember that you can't change other people; you can only change yourself. Instead of trying to make difficult people change, ask yourself, 'Why am I so vulnerable in this area? What are my blind spots? How could I handle myself better with such people?'

- Resist the temptation to label other people
  Practise observing and describing what other people feel, think, say and do. Call them negative names when you want to swear and positive ones when you want to put them on a pedestal – but recognise that the labels you are using reflect your emotional state, not them.

- Take time to stand and stare
  Pause occasionally to observe what is happening in situations that you find yourself in. Take several deep breaths. Scan your feelings. Be alert to fleeting impressions; notice the small things and be alert to early clues about what may be going on.

- Be your own best friend
  Take time to appreciate yourself for the things that you do. Appreciate your accomplishments and give yourself a pat on the back when you help someone. Maintaining your feelings of positive self-regard helps take the edge off hurtful criticism. Your self-esteem

> determines how much you learn after something goes wrong. If you are busy protecting yourself from hurt you will not be open to learning. So, the stronger your self-esteem, the more you will learn.
>
> - When bad times come along follow the survivor sequence
>   Regain your emotional balance, adapt and cope with the immediate situation, thrive by learning and being creative, then find the gift. The better you become, the faster you can turn disaster into good fortune.

AND SO TO END . . .

Now we have finally reached the end of the journey I hope you have learnt some useful ways to confront life's difficulties and turn them around. I hope, too, that what you have read has enabled you to appreciate that although difficult experiences cannot always be avoided, going through adversity can lead you to discover the power that lies within. This chapter isn't quite the end of the book, but it is where I bow out. The next section is devoted to the words of survivors themselves. I hope their stories will give you some inspiration and enable you to develop your own ways to survive.

PART THREE
INSPIRATIONS AND INFORMATION

CHAPTER TWELVE
INSPIRING PEOPLE AND BOOKS

The survivors here have been through some of life's most painful hardships – painful relationships, being deserted by parents, child abuse, emotional abuse, relationship break up, and job loss. Some of them make difficult reading, so do so only when you feel ready. You may want to pick a moment when you are feeling strong. Alternatively, you may find that reading how other people survived when you are feeling weak helps you gain new strength. The key factor in these accounts is that they all learnt how to survive in their own way. There is no one recipe for survival. Some of the ways the people here survived and their insights might be right for you, others you may reject. The important thing is to remember that they did survive and so can you.

- 'Being made redundant did me a big favour'
  Sylvia Hutton, job club leader

  Sylvia was 45 when she was made redundant from her job as accounts administrator in the chartered surveyor's office of an Edwardian estate. She had no inkling that she was to be made redundant. Someone was sent down from head office to break the news. She was given three months' notice. The first emotion Sylvia felt was disbelief. 'At first I even felt sorry for him. He didn't handle it lightly and I remember thinking, "I bet you'd rather be *anywhere else than here telling me this." I made it easy for him.'* Her initial disbelief soon gave way to anger, but *'I didn't express my annoyance. I wish now I had.'*

When she went home, Sylvia remembers she treated it *'quite lightly: I truly believed it was their loss and I do believe, as I tell the people who come to the job club: "You're not redundant, the job is." Even so I couldn't help thinking at my age . . .'*

Sylvia believes that in some ways losing her job was her own fault. She was too efficient. In her previous job in a building society she had been used to *'rushing around here there and everywhere.'* She couldn't stand not having enough to do. She always believed that she would get work, and so it proved. However, there were times when she felt she lost her confidence when she went for a couple of job interviews and didn't get the jobs. *'I remember one I thought had gone well, I spent the whole day being interviewed. I knew I could do the job, but I also suspected that it would be given to one of the other candidates. When they told me I hadn't got the job I just said, "Oh, thank you," which isn't at all like me. I did believe however that it wasn't my fault.'*

During the three months in which she worked her notice Sylvia contacted all the people she knew — friends and former employers. *'I even toyed with the idea of applying to an ex-manager I knew, because I knew I would get a job there. However I didn't really want that, so I kept it as a last resort.'*

Throughout the three months she kept quite light-hearted. However, *'deep down I was quite frightened.'* She was frightened of losing her living standard because she had already given up full-time work to work part-time and *'we were only just coping then.'* She also feared her age was against her.

Fortunately, Sylvia managed to find a job through a friend. She was relieved to get a job, but feels the experience of being made redundant did bring positive gains. *'It makes you see things in a different light, as does the job I am now doing. I feel I have more empathy with people now who have no job. I was lucky. My attitude towards people who were out of work changed. I didn't used to give them a great deal of thought. Now I do.'*

Being made redundant affects all your relationships. Sylvia has a good friend whose husband has been out of work for a long time. She had always wondered how they made ends meet and how she would cope in that situation. 'I used to think a lot about that. It puts you on your guard. You don't like to say to someone in that situation that you are going on holiday, for example. It's awful when you come back with a sun tan. You want to talk about your holiday, but you don't like to.'

She believes she survived the loss of her job by taking it lightly and being prepared to do a variety of jobs. 'I knew I had experience and transferable skills and I used to try and put over that I would be a good employee and a reliable person.'

Sylvia knows that she comes over as confident, but she said, 'It doesn't always mean you are inside.' However, she said she did feel in control and that she had choices. She was helped by the fact that her family and friends had confidence in her.

Today she still worries about being out of work. However, she feels confident because she has survived it once. She said, 'It's a cliché but it's true that as one door closes another opens. I'm far happier and more involved in what I do today. In a way being made redundant did me a big favour.'

- *'You have to get on, don't dwell on the past and make your future.'*

    Lucy Chatsworth, interior designer

Lucy was the middle child of three, with an older sister and a younger brother. Her family moved around a lot as her father was in the Armed Services. Her family was incredibly loving and she felt loved by both parents. However she was adored by her father and criticised by her mother who was, 'very proper in many ways.'

Her childhood was 'fine in parts but difficult in others.' She found it especially hard being sent away to boarding school at 11 as the discipline was hard to take. 'What I am saying is that there was no big event or crisis in my childhood or adolescence that triggered my disastrous relationship.'

Looking back, however, Lucy sees how strong and important her parents' 'dynamic' was on her. 'To my Dad I was the apple of his eye, we all were. He made us feel special, capable and interesting. My Mum, on the other hand, all good meals and lovely clothes, just didn't come through with the warmth. She was always ill or martyrish somehow. I'm sure she resented my Dad's love for us and his love for life. She was the "dutiful" one and I can see now that we were never allowed to forget it.'

When Lucy was 29 she met a man through a friend who was 'something out of a novel: good-looking, suave, rich.' They flirted all evening, and he asked to see her again. When she said, 'Yes,' he said, 'You shouldn't have said that. Never give the game away.' She thought he was just being funny and in fact they did go out. The times they spent together were always really intense and exciting: 'flash meals, trips, sex on Hampstead Heath, in the back of cars.' However, there was always 'an edge'. Lucy could tell that he was always playing games. And, in fact, she now realises 'playing with me.'

Nevertheless, she still fell for him. 'I fell under his spell in a way and began to see the world through his eyes, which was odd as his views were extreme.' She described him as being like 'a pioneer. Lone man with his possessions, Me, against the world.' She believes that at this point she was just infatuated and addicted to the excitement and danger that he offered. He was a 'wheeler-dealer' and she soon realised that 'nothing was as it seemed, and that somehow made him more exotic.'

Lucy thought her upbringing played a big part in that it helped her keep a sense of 'normality and propriety' when all else was failing. However, it was also the reason she was so attracted to him. 'It was like a life preserver, yet it kept me bound.'

Eventually, she became pregnant and he expected her to give up her work and her life in order to bring up 'his' child (in fact children – she has two). 'I genuinely think for him he had what he wanted. But he had also won. He had taken my life from me.'

It was at this point that he started to become violent. At first it was subtle: sex was rough and he used to order her around. Then he started to humiliate her when people were around, 'Either by being outrageously sexual or lewd at my expense. Or by pointing out my failures and calling me names. Even as this was going on I was making excuses for him, finding ways to explain his behaviour.'

Lucy's family were horrified, but in a way they were powerless, as were her friends, as she was still supporting her partner's behaviour. She said, 'I think in the beginning I didn't realise how he was altering my values. I am appalled now when I think how arrogant and stupid I was to ignore the help of my family and friends and their insight into my situation over the years.'

She felt things were like an increasing nightmare as she became ever more embroiled with a man who was patently dishonest to the point of being criminal and becoming ever more abusive.

Finally he started beating her up in public and in front of her children. That was the turning point. 'I think sometimes you have to go quite far down a road before you realise you have taken a wrong turning. You keep hoping it will be the right way. Also I am a stubborn person. I was used to trusting my instinct so it was hard for me to admit I had made a mistake.'

Lucy said her view of life had changed. She now realised that 'you can't always play with fire and expect to stay unscathed. Before, I had enjoyed that.' She had also changed her views about her upbringing and for the first time in her life realised how angry she was with certain people. 'Maybe that relationship was about being surrounded by anger to such a point that I had to free my own.'

She believed she was a survivor but also that, 'My view of people will never be quite the same.' However, she is determined for her own sake and that of her children not to let her experience poison her. 'He was sick and there are people out there in disguise. But you have to hope that you will spot them, or that they are not in your lot.'

She wouldn't go to therapy as she feels she has survived and 'It is down to me now, not for anyone else to show me the path.' She believed that, 'You have to get on, don't dwell on the past and make your future.' She has always been quite practical and she thinks that is one of the things that has enabled her to survive.

Today, she has a new partner and she said she was optimistic about the future. 'I am definitely an optimist at heart. In fact I can't really imagine what pessimism feels like. It's not that hard to create things that are good enough and then work upwards from there. To start off expecting the worst and having to get over that feels too much of a task on a daily basis.'

- 'The skill is to keep going.'
  Ricardo D'Gama, healer and holistic masseur

Ricardo came from a family of six children. His mother divorced his father when he was about one. She had met someone else who became her partner although she did not marry. He had no interest in the five children that Ricardo's mother brought into the relationhip, so he was brought up with no fathering whatsoever. This led to him being 'very self-sufficient and working things out myself.'

His mother's partner related to Ricardo through getting him to do things and violence. 'He was really strict, had a drink problem that was not acknowledged to himself and related to me through the belt and a heavy hand. His big thing was that you had to tell the truth.' Richard remembers clearly telling lies as the truth was not good enough. He was physically abused and his mother was scared.

Ricardo's mother received little financial support from her partner so she was forced to get two jobs. 'She was scared of him and scared of him walking out and leaving her with six kids to bring up.' If his mother hadn't stayed with this man they would definitely have gone into care, because she wouldn't have been able to look after them.

His mother made sure they were clothed and that there was always food on the table and occasional treats and that was as much as she could give. She couldn't give emotional support or a listening ear. 'I developed a stance of "I'll keep my stuff to myself." I witnessed him being violent to others. He was a disciplinarian and had a warped way of thinking.'

Ricardo believes he got his self-sufficiency from his mother and his real father and that he had to learn it. Self-sufficiency meant having a job from the age of 10, and doing lots of practical things such as making the family's tea, as his mother would be working. He believes he developed emotional self-sufficiency very early. 'I can remember many thrashings and never once talking about it. I'd just go to my bedroom and cry myself to sleep and forget it, in the sense that I would think, "Oh, it's normal. It's OK."'

He believed that being self-sufficient had given him enormous strength. 'When I have to do something I initially feel very vulnerable and then that makes me know I can do it, as I can draw on these massive resources. If I have a resistance to doing something, I'll do it.'

For many years, though, Ricardo felt his self-sufficiency held him back, 'If I had had a lever: a mother or father saying "What's wrong? You can do this or that", it might have been different. It's interesting to me thinking how my son will be as he will have levers and support.'

Intuition is a strong attribute. Ricardo was literally brought up on the street in gangs. He believed he must have trusted himself as he got into all sorts of life-threatening situations: drink, drugs, thieving and fights. At one time his brother was in a detention centre and there was a strong possibility that Ricardo would follow him. He went to court and it frightened the life out of him: 'That was a changing point.'

His intuition has helped him know what was right for him to do. 'It's almost as if there is a computer inside me, which I call my "self" as I am self-taught. I hear myself saying, "If you do that, these are the consequences. This is what may well happen.' And then I get a feeling that comes over me that says," That's right! That's what I want to do."'

He believed that at one level coming from the background he has done has been 'incredibly positive'. Really difficult and painful. But working through that and understanding that the pain has to be met and healed and shared, it then becomes an incredible resource.'

Trust was a key word for Ricardo. At one time he drove taxis but he gave that up to train as an alternative therapist. He trusted himself to leave the world of being a cabbie and go into complementary therapy. 'It was an all or nothing situation. It was like in the house I grew up in. Do or die.'

When he was 17 he had 'a kind of breakdown'. He had been attempting to escape his distress by taking refuge in drugs. 'I went into my room and I just wept without knowing why.' *He had never believed in God, but he looked in that direction and 'found something.' After this, he came across a book on meditation and yoga and this helped him a great deal.*

'I did yoga and meditation every day and it was amazing. It altered my perceptions and I realised how sensitive I was and began to understand a lot more about my relationships.' *He also met a healer and this was a profound experience which led to him getting to know his real father.* 'I realised that I needed to get to know him, and that it was very painful and I will never get over it, but now I know about him and I understand.'

Through Jungian psychotherapy he made the decision to sever the relationship with his father as it was 'preventing me from going on.'. *He had to accept that he hadn't and wasn't going to be fathered. And now he was about to be a father himself.* 'This was crucial inner work that has enabled me to father my child. What is very important is that you don't re-enact. It's a constant battle.'

Ricardo said 'the skill is to keep going.' *He believed he met everything initially with pessimism and this was positive as* 'it opens up why I'm looking negatively at something.' *This then allows him to create something positive and experience things more fully.* 'It's all or nothing again. It's like Goethe said, "Boldness has genius, power, magic in it. Begin it now." In the end I think about life "If I'm going to do it, do it." Otherwise, there's no point in being here.'

- *'You need to accept who you are and feel forgiving'*
  Brenda Nicholls, artist

Brenda's mother gave her and her sister away for adoption when she was three and her sister was one. She said, 'I don't think she had any problem with doing that, as I genuinely think she can never have wanted us in the first place'. Brenda's 'parents' told her she was adopted when she was about nine, and after the shock it was a relief as she had always felt very different from her 'family'. She doesn't think that her sister felt the same sense of difference as she was that much younger.

After this intial relief, however, came feelings of hurt and rejection and the need to know 'why and who could have done this to me. I became obsessed with wanting to meet my mum.' Eventually, when Brenda was 12, Social Services set up a meeting. She remembers feeling sick and excited. 'My mum just sat there when me and my sister were shown into the room. She didn't get up, kiss us or anything. She just asked us if we were alright, but not like in the movies where that could be seen as sad and meaningful. She was just uninterested and couldn't think of anything else to say.'

After the interview, Brenda felt desperate and asked if she could see her mother again. But her mother said, 'No.' After this Brenda went 'sort of mad'. She stopped eating, drank a lot and then started cutting herself, first on her arms and then on her stomach. 'It was weird, horrific but pleasurable.' She remembers feeling afraid that she would cut herself when she was alone in her room at night and then feeling good when she did. She had to become 'a loner of sorts' so no one would see the cuts. She couldn't go swimming, have sex or care what she wore in case people saw. 'I think my family thought I was weired but "That was teenagers for you".' By then, she had stopped communicating with her family and she thinks that she hated them for adopting her. 'I hated myself so much. I felt so different from everybody, like I was an outcast and it was all my fault, as my mum had not loved me enough to want me.'

Brenda believes that being the older child both helped and hindered her survival. She never talked to her sister as she wanted to protect her, and she believes that in some way this protective role gave her a reason to live. By the time she was 18, she was desperate to move away from home and went to art college. 'That was good in that nobody minds if you are a mad artist. But equally no one asks you why you paint the way you do,' so she was still alone and still cutting herself.

She had 'sort of crappy attempts at love affairs that were hopeless and abusive.' And then she met an older student, a woman, who for some reason she told about the cutting. To Brenda's amazement, she handled this knowledge and talked to Brenda. 'It was as if years of agony suddenly became real rather than hidden.' It was to be several years before Brenda went into therapy but she doesn't think she could ever have done that if she had not told the woman at art school.

Today, Brenda says she is still not a happy person and she doesn't think that the feeling of rejection will ever leave her. However, she says, 'Now I think "why should it?" After all I was rejected. That is my truth. And so I do damage limitation when I can. I see that I was the victim of someone else's mistake – not the cause or reason of it.'

She feels her pessimism is her ally. 'It doesn't usually let you down, and when it does it's OK, as something better than you hoped for happened. I do think of myself as a survivor and as someone who is just surviving and I think that is real.'

'I don't know who I would have been if I hadn't been left. I suspect I would have still been serious as I need to think about things. I think that is a technique. It can drive you mad, but it can get you through, if you just keep thinking. Life isn't simple. You need to accept that. But more than that, you have to accept who you are and feel forgiving – not to people who treat you badly necessarily, but to yourself.'

- *'It happened. . . . Life here I come.'*
  Betty Westgate, MBE

Betty, founder and president of the charity Breast Cancer Care, was 49 in 1968 and the head of a biology department at a school, when she discovered a breast lump. Betty went to her GP who gave her the phone numbers of three hospitals and told her to get the earliest appointment she could. She remembers 'The consultant who came round with his tribe of students, examined me and said he thought it was nothing at all. However, he suggested I should have the lump removed.' In those days, time was not considered to be such an important factor and it was seven weeks before Betty had a biopsy. She was told that the lump was 'nothing' and she and her husband went out to celebrate. Unfortunately it did not turn out to be 'nothing' – a week later Betty received a phone call telling her the lump was cancerous. 'My first reaction was one of horror. There was very little information about breast cancer in those days and since my mother, who was living with us at the time, considered the disease a desperate sentence, I found it very difficult to cope with. Having been told it was nothing seemed to make the diagnosis twice as bad.' Eight days after the diagnosis, Betty had a mastectomy (breast removal), the standard treatment for breast cancer at that time, and believed that would be the last of it. 'In my ignorance, that removed the problem.' It was only when she went to visit one of her daughters-in-law, Rosemary, who had just had her second baby, that she discovered her troubles were by no means over. The doctor visiting Rosemary told Betty, 'Women can survive ten years after breast cancer.' Her first thought was, 'Why did I bother with surgery?' But in the car going home she felt a tremendous anger which was focused on the bearer of the bad news. 'I thought, "Damn you, I'm not just going to survive, I'm going to live for a further 30 years".' 27 years later she is, as she says, 'Applying for an extension!' She feels that the flash of anger she experienced had helped her, together with a lifelong habit of being optimistic.

When she returned to work, Betty found that a lot of people were generally very negative about cancer. 'Many colleagues *seemed to find it difficult to talk to me with their previous ease. I also noticed that acquaintances would go into shops or cross the road rather than meet me. At first I felt hurt and shunned — then I realised fear was causing this behaviour. Many equated cancer with death and didn't know what to say to me.'*

As a result Betty formed an organisation, the Cancer Education Service, early in 1972. Drawing on her previous experience as a school teacher and as a Samaritan, she went out into the community and talked to people about cancer. She met a lot of women who had had mastectomies who felt their needs were not being met, and from this feeling grew the Mastectomy Association (now Breast Cancer Care) in 1973, five years after her own cancer was diagnosed. She feels that she has a survivor mentality and that a big part of this comes from her own temperament. *'If people are naturally emotional it can be more difficult. It's easier if you are more stoical and think, "It happened. . . . Life here I come."'* However she does recognise that *'It's not that easy to switch off one set of emotions and switch on another.'* She believes in the power of talk to help people to come to terms with breast cancer. *'I was lucky that at first I thought my lump was nothing. When I discovered it was something, I was somehow able to draw on those positive feelings I had previously felt when I thought it was nothing. At the same time, my mother was so terrified of breast cancer that I couldn't have upset her, so I was able to put it behind me.'*

She believes another part of her survival kit is her determination. *'I have always been the sort of person who, if they know they want something, will go out and get it.'* She recalls how, at the age of 18, she had a keen desire to learn to fly, so she obtained a post at her local flying club and, in return for working there, was able to train as a pilot. Similarly she trained to teach when she was in her 30s despite having four sons.

Like most survivors, Betty says, *'I have always been a great planner for the future. If my thoughts started to wander, I'd always switch them back to something more positive. I remember, one day after I had the mastectomy, seeing a blue dress that I liked in a* shop window and thinking, "What's the use?" I was so horrified to find myself thinking this, that I went straight into the shop and bought it. I still have that dress hanging in my wardrobe.' She says, 'Everybody has negative thoughts – it's a question of confronting and trying to overcome them.' She feels her four sons also kept her going. 'I had all their futures to think about and I think that helped. If you are alone, it must be that much more difficult to deal with your problems.' She laughs as she recalls one method she had of switching off her negative thoughts. 'I would take a Yeastvite (vitamin supplement). My mother had a great belief in them and I suppose I picked it up from her. I'm not sure how much actual good they did, but the point is I was doing something active to master my feelings.' Another important part of her survival armoury was the support of her husband and family. 'My husband has always been very positive so I was only carrying my own load and some of that could be shared with him. He gave me his full support, not just the odd five minutes here and there.'

FURTHER READING

A great many books are now available to help people learn more about themselves, take action and enhance their lives. Among the ones I have found most useful are:

- **General survival**
  Breaking Free From Your Past. Carolyn Foster, Headway (Hodder and Stoughton)
  Staying OK. Amy and Thomas Harris, Pan
  Superconfidence. Gael Lindenfield, Thorsons
  Living with Change. Ursula Markham, Element
  The Road Less Travelled. M. Scott Peck, Arrow
  Healing Grief. Barbara Ward, Vermilion
- **Surviving feelings**
  Feeling Good. The New Mood Therapy, David D. Burns, Signet
  OK 2 Talk Feelings. Dr Jenny Cozens, BBC Books
  Breaking the Bonds. Dorothy Rowe, Fontana
- **Surviving relationships**
  Changing hearts. Jill Burrett, Allen and Unwin
  When Love Goes Wrong. Ann Jones and Susan Schechter, Victor Gollancz
  Letting Go of Loneliness. Gina Levete, Element
  The Relate Guide to Better Relationships. Sarah Litvinoff, Ebury Press
  Sexual Power. Sandra Sedgbeer, Thorsons
  Equal Partners. Tina B Tessina and Riley K Smith, Headway (Hodder and Stoughton)
- **Surviving work**
  What Colour is Your Parachute. Richard Nelson Bolles, Ten Speed Press
  The Daily Telegraph. Changing your job after 35. Godfrey Golzen and Philip Plumbley, Kogan Page
  Going Freelance. Godfrey Golzen, Kogan Page
  Finding the Right Job. Anne Segall with William Greason, BBC Books
  Goodbye 9–5. Michael Syrett, New Opportunity Press

- **Surviving illness**
  Mind Over Medicine. Robin Blake, Pan
  The Health Care Consumer Guide. Robert Gann, Faber and Faber
  How to Survive Medical Treatment, Dr Stephen Fulder, CW Daniel
  Pleasing the Patient. Geoff Watts, Faber and Faber

Appendix 1
WHO CAN HELP?

Although this book has been mainly about how to develop the qualities you need to help you survive on your own, there may be times when professional help, in the form of psychotherapy, can be useful. For people suffering from phobias (such as agoraphobia or obsessive-compulsive disorder), for example, exposure therapy has been shown to be more successful than drugs in helping people to confront their fears and anxieties. Brief cognitive therapy (see below) has also proved to be as effective as drugs in helping those who are suffering from depression.

It's not, however, a good idea to rush into psychotherapy the moment disaster strikes. Many experts even believe we are running the danger of 'medicalising' normal, everyday problems which, given time, would ease anyway. Professor John Pearce, a psychiatrist who heads the Department of Child and Adolescent Psychiatry at Nottingham University, says, 'It worries me that the automatic response when anything adverse occurs is the desire for counselling or therapy. The mind has its own mechanisms for coping wit natural stresses such as death, illness or disaster. By rushing into psychotherapy, people fail to recognise the natural healing process that is present in all of us.'

Professor Pearce also argues that much psychoanalytic theory – which involves delving deeply in the past and your childhood (see below) – doesn't actually work. 'What people need most is a problem-solving approach using coping strategies rather than insight. And in some ways, just as picking at a physical scab can reopen a healing wound, constantly letting off emotional steam can actually make matters worse.'

Worse still are the stories of therapists who abuse their power by seducing their patients. Surveys show that an alarmingly high number of therapists have had sex with their patients. This applies to both medically trained and non-medically trained therapists.

Even more alarming is the so-called 'false memory syndrome', where people are believed to have been persuaded by therapists to imagine falsely that they have been the victims of sexual abuse as children. According to the American clinical psychologist Dr Michael Yapko, a 'startling proportion' of therapists are leading their patients to make such claims. 'I am deeply concerned that psychotherapy patients will be led to believe destructive ideas that are untrue, recall memories of events that never happened, jump to conclusions that are not warranted and destroy the lives of innocent people.' However Marjorie Orr, of Accuracy About Abuse, an organisation designed to expose the incidence and damaging results of childhood sexual abuse, cautions against throwing out the baby with the bath water. 'Undoubtedly there is a lunatic fringe and there is some bad therapy. But there's not a scrap of evidence to suggest that therapists fill people's heads with false fantasies. There's always a reason why people have those particular fantasies. And although I'm sure there are false allegations, they are not false memories. Most people do remember abuse, and if they have forgotten it's because they're not ready to remember. The whole business has been deeply damaging to therapy, and has caused deep distress to real abuse survivors who are often frightened to disclose the abuse and don't know whether to believe themselves anyway.'

So how can you avoid the pitfalls? When might therapy be appropriate? And what should people be looking for in a therapist? The British Mental Health Foundation is setting up a Psychotherapy Research Initiative designed to evaluate the various types of psychotherapy, investigate the competence of therapists, and see whether it is cost-effective. In the meantime I would advise you not to rush into therapy and to bear in mind the time scale of the natural healing process: after any adverse event an average two weeks of feeling devastated or numb, and up to six weeks of acute pain, are experienced. By six months to a year, though problems may still be felt, a person should be on their feet again. Before seeking professional help, think who else you could talk to among your friends, relatives and those close to you. Finally, if you're told anything by a therapist that makes you feel uneasy, don't automatically assume the therapist is right and you are wrong. As clinical psychologist and author Dorothy Rose observes, 'A good therapist is someone who listens, asks you questions and gives positive support, but doesn't give advice or issue instructions. A bad therapist tells you what to do and makes you feel worse.'

TYPES OF THERAPY

- **Psychoanalysis**
  The granddad of all psychotherapies, Freud, first invented this method of treatment. The patient lies on a couch and talks while the therapist listens. It may also involve dream work and delving around in the person's subconscious and childhood. This therapy can go on for many years. Although it may provide a lot of insight, this approach has largely been discredited as a way of dealing with specific problems, such as depression.
- **Behaviour therapy**
  This concentrates on changing the way we behave rather than focusing on thoughts and the subconscious. This therapy has proved extremely useful for phobias, for example. In such cases, it might involve gradually exposing sufferers to the feared situation until it becomes so familiar that it no longer holds any anxiety for the sufferer. This is also known as exposure therapy.
- **Cognitive therapy**
  This is designed to help the patient understand how negative ways of thinking can distort perceptions and cause problems. The therapy aims to uncover unhelpful ways of thinking and to replace them with more positive ones. It's been particularly successful in treating depression. Cognitive therapy may also be combined with behaviour (cognitive behavioural therapy) and psychoanalytic (cognitive analytic therapy) techniques.

- **Counselling**
  Counselling is less intensive than psychotherapy but involves a similar process of looking at patterns of behaviour and trying to relate them to previous events in a person's life. Counselling can help develop the inner resources needed to cope with a problem and is often specific (marriage counselling or bereavement counselling, for example).

FINDING A THERAPIST

One of the biggest problems in finding a therapist is that, at present, there is little regulation or guidance in psychotherapy. 'It's all too easy to train as a psychotherapist,' says Stephen White of the British Psychological Society. 'There's no statutory national register of psychotherapists. There are no minimum training requirements, and little explanation of the various therapies and what they are intended to do. And while a psychiatrist is a medical doctor who has undergone additional training in mental health, including psychotherapy, there's no legal definition of the terms "psychotherapist" or "psychologist".'

There is, however, some progress being made. The UK Council of Psychotherapy has a register listing some 3,000 names. In order to be listed, therapists have to train or be accredited by one of 74 strictly screened organisations belonging to the council. The British Association of Counselling has a list of 660 members who are accredited. Both these have codes of practice and complaints procedures, as of course do psychiatrists and clinical psychologists (psychologists who work within medicine). However, this still leaves literally thousands of psychotherapists who aren't medically qualified and belong to no such organisations.

Of course, just because someone belongs to one of these organisations, this doesn't guarantee that he or she will be a good therapist. But at least, if you do choose an accredited therapist, there is some comeback should things go wrong. As Dorothy Rowe points out, 'There are bad therapists among those who are medically qualified as well as those who have no training to speak of.' At the end of the day, what really counts is the personal chemistry between you and your therapist. This puts the onus on you to check a therapist out before you go to see them. Always remember that if a therapist makes you feel worse, it's not you who's wrong and change your therapist. A good therapist should follow certain basic rules. It's your right to be believed, valued and supported, and to know that what you say is confidential. Use the following checklist to help you find someone who can help you.

> **Finding a therapist checklist**
>
> 1. A therapist should never start telling you about his or her own personal problems, or compare your problems with his or hers. Even situations that seem superficially similar on the surface are in fact completely different.
>
> 2. Beware of any therapist who appears to be trying to put words into your mouth or plant recollections of traumatic events, such as sexual abuse, by asking leading questions. A therapist should give you time to tell your own story, in your own way.
>
> 3. A therapist should never tell you directly what to do. The idea of therapy is to help you to find your own solutions.
>
> 4. Needless to say, a therapist should never try to touch you in a sexual way, ask you to undress or talk to you suggestively.
>
> 5. Beware of a counsellor who believes in keeping a family together at all costs, despite significant problems such as physical or sexual abuse, deteriorating health and mental well-being.
>
> 6. Beware of any therapist who doesn't believe you, suggests that your problems are all your own fault, blames you for abuse, or suggests that you 'get something out of it'.

7. Steer clear of any therapist who doesn't make you feel cared for, encouraged, and supported, or who actively humiliates or criticises you.

8. If you still don't trust your therapist, or feel safe with him or her, even after several sessions, or if your therapist gossips about what you have said, stop seeing him or her immediately.

9. If, even after working together for months, you see absolutely no change in yourself or feel you are not learning anything new, then the therapy has not been successful and you should think about looking elsewhere.

10. Beware of any therapist who promises an instant fix – especially if the therapist has a hobby horse (such as a particular religion), or type of therapy (such as hypnosis). Most longstanding problems will take some time to sort out.

11. Beware of any therapist who tries to extort large sums of money from you up front. A good therapist will make any financial involvement on your part very clear from the start.

Appendix 2
USEFUL ADDRESSES

- **Surviving addictions**

  Alcoholics Anonymous
  PO Box 1
  Stonebow House
  Stonebow
  York YO1 2NJ
  01904 644026 (Head office; local numbers in telephone directory)

  Gambler's Anonymous
  PO Box 88
  London SW10 0EU
  0171 384 3040

  Quitline (help for people who want to stop smoking)
  Victory House
  170 Tottenham Court Road
  London W1P 0HA
  0171 487 3000

- **Surviving childhood**

  British Agencies for Adoption and Fostering
  Skyline House
  200 Union Street
  London SE1 0LY
  0171 593 2000

  Childwatch (Help for adults who were abused as children)
  206 Hessle Road
  Hull HU3 3BE
  01482 216681

NSPCC (National Society for the Prevention of Cruelty to Children)
42 Curtain Road
London EC2A 3NH
0171 825 2500

- **Surviving bereavement**

  Child Death Helpline
  c/o Bereavement services co-ordinator
  The Hospital for Sick Children
  Great Ormond Street
  London WC1N 3JH
  0171 829 8685

  Cruse – Bereavement Care
  Cruse House
  126 Sheen Road
  Richmond
  Surrey TW9 1UR
  0181 940 4818

  Foundation for the Study of Infant Deaths
  35 Belgrave Square
  London SW1X 8QB
  0171 235 1721

  SANDS (Stillbirth and Neonatal Death Society)
  28 Portland Place
  London W1N 4DE
  0171 436 5881

- **Surviving a break up**

  British Association of Counselling (BACS)
  1 Regent Place
  Rugby
  Warks CV21 2PJ
  01788 578328

British Association for Sexual and Marital Therapy
PO Box 63
Sheffield
South Yorks S10 3TS

Catholic Marriage Advisory Council
Clitherow House
1 Blythe Mews
Blythe Road
London W14 0NW
0171 371 1341

Relate – National Marriage Guidance
Herbert Gray College
Little Church Street
Rugby
Warks CV21 3AP
01788 573241

- **Surviving cancer**

Breast Cancer Care
15–19 Britten Street
London SW3 3TZ
01500 245345 (helpline)

BACUP (British Association of Cancer United Patients)
3 Bath Place
Rivington Street
London EC2A 3JR
0171 613 2121 (helpline)

- **Surviving eating disorders**

Eating Disorders Association
Sackville Place
44 Magdalen Street
Norwich NR3 1JU
01603 621414

- **Surviving job loss**

    CEPEC (Centre for Professional Employment Counselling)
    67 Jermyn Street,
    London SW1Y 6NY
    0171 930 0322

    Focus (Forum for Occupational Counselling and Unemployment)
    Northside House
    Mount Pleasant
    Barnet
    Herts EN4 9EB
    0181 441 9300

- **Surviving parenthood**

    Cry-sis (self-help and support for families with excess crying, sleeplessness and demanding children)
    BM Cry-sis
    London WC1N 3XX
    0171 404 5011

    Parentline (self help and support for parents under stress)
    57 Hart Road
    Thundersley
    Essex SS7 3PD
    01268 757077

- **Surviving pregnancy**

    Miscarriage Association
    c/o Clayton Hospital
    Northgate
    Wakefield
    W Yorks WF1 3JS
    01921 200700

National Childbirth Trust
Alexandra House
Oldham Terrace
London W3 6NH
0181 992 8637

SATFA (Support Around Termination for Abnormality)
29–30 Soho Square
London W1V 6JB
0171 439 6124

- **Surviving sickness**

  Association of Community Health Councils for England and Wales (information about your rights when you are ill)
  30 Drayton Park
  London N5 1PB

  Patients Association
  18 Victoria Park Square
  Bethnal Green
  London E2 9PF
  0181 981 5676

- **Surviving terminal illness**

  Hospice Information Service
  51–59 Lawrie Park Road
  Sydenham
  London SE26 6DZ
  0181 778 9252

- **Surviving violence and abuse**

  Rape Crisis Centre
  PO Box 69
  London WC1X 9NJ
  0171 837 1600

Victim Support
Cranmer House
39 Brixton Road
London SW9 6DZ
0171 735 9166

Women's Aid Federation for England (for abused women)
PO Box 391
Bristol BS99 7WS
0117 963 3542

- **Surviving mental illness**

MIND – National Association for Mental Health
Granta House
15–19 Broadway
Stratford
London E15 4BQ
0181 519 2122 or 0171 637 0741

SANE (Schizophrenia – A National Emergency)
2nd Floor
199–205 Old Marylebone Road
London NW1 5QP
0171 724 6520

- **For further information about self-help groups**

National Council for Voluntary Organisations
Regent's Wharf
8 All Saints Street
London N1 9RL
0171 713 6161

INDEX

abilities, mental *see* intelligence
abuse 182, 194
   childhood sexual 160
acupuncture 380
agendas, hidden 64
alcohol 37
anger 118, 151, 152, 181 *see also* emotions
anorexia 149
anxiety 36, 37
asthma 30
attitudes, negative 24
awareness, emotional 48
   kinaesthetic 79
   see also emotions

backache 30
barriers, mental 87
   to survival 85, 87
bereavement *see* death; grief
body, language 29–30
   listening to the 64
Bowlby, John 171
brain 77
break-ups *see* relationships
breathing techniques 47
burn-out 34

caffeine 36
cancer 32
cataracts 32
challenge 83
change 16, 26, 91, 100–3, 108–9, 183 *see also* turning points
   cycle of 18, 110, 125
   in health, *see* health, changes in
   in relationship *see* relationships, break-up of; difficulties in
   thriving in the face of 80
chemistry of the moment 94

child, inner 95
children 169 *see also* relationships, with children
cognitive therapy, *see* therapy, cognitive
compulsive eating 30
communication 49 *see also* emotions, expression of
confidence 10, 53 *see also* self-confidence
control, emotional 46–7
cost-benefit analysis 115
creativity 78
crises 23
   life 161
   management of 24
curiosity 41

death 151–2, 156
   of partner 156
   of baby or child 157
   accidental 157
   cot 157
   see also grief
defence mechanisms 85–7
denial 117
dependency 115 *see also* partner, controlling
depression 54, 107, 141, 152
development, emotional 41
   mental 78
diabetes 32
disaster 155–167
disfigurement 145
drinking 30
drugs, non-prescribed 30

emotions 10, 41–58, 117–20
   balance of 56
   dealing with 161–3

expression of 41, 49
fighting against 55
release of 50–1, 119
transformation of 51–2
see also awareness, emotional;
   energy, emotional
empathy 60, 62, 66, 135, 143, 173, 190
endorphins 32, 38
energy, emotional 41
   mental 30, 36–5
   physical 30, 36
exercise 32

fatigue 33, 37
feelings *see* emotions
Ferguson, Marilyn 77
flexibility 19, 68, 77, 103, 169, 183
friendship *see* relationships

gift, finding the 163, 165
Golzen, Godfrey 128
grief 117
   guidelines 158–60
   stages of 129
guilt 117, 161

habits, bad 37
Hay, Louise 150
headache 30, 103
health, changes in 137–54
   holistic 137
heart disease 31
heart rate 32
helplessness 118 *see also*
   emotions; dependency
Hitchcock, Alfred 171
hospital, stay in 146
humour, graveyard 88
   sense of 10, 102, 166, 180
hypnosis 38

illness, terminal 152 *see also*
   health, changes in; death
image, personal 39
immune system, emotional 16

immunity, physical 15
insomnia 37
intelligence 77–80
intuition 16, 28, 195

job, loss of 125–36
   finding a new 131–6
   interviews 134–6

languages, speaking foreign 79
Levinson, Daniel 94
Lieberman, Morton 19
life tasks 93, 97–100
   check 96
   crisis *see* crisis, life
   plan 97
listening skills *see* skills, listening
loneliness 107 *see also* depression
loss 149 *see also* death; grief; job, loss of
love 107

marriage 176
meditation 47, 119, 147, 196
medicine, complementary 139
messages, unhelpful 45
migraine *see* headaches
miscarriage *see* death of baby or child
Miscarriage Association 158 *see also* SANDS
mourning 156 *see also* death; grief
myths, survival 76

Norcross, John 16
Nursing Times 161
nutrition 31

pain, emotional 16, 30
   physical 30
parenthood 96
partner, controlling 60, 116
   death of *see* death, of partner
past, influence of the 30
Patients Association, The 147
Peck, Dr M. Scott 16

people, dealing with angry 70
  difficult 65, 68
  negative 68
perception, styles of 62–3
pessimism, 46, 194, 196, 198
plans 172 *see also* life, plan
Plumbley, Philip 128
psychotherapy, cognitive 39

redundancy 189
reflexes 4
relaxation 33–4, 38, 47
relationships,
  break-up of, 110–15
  with children 120–3
  difficulties in 108–24, 192
  doctor/patient 142
  with friends 172, 177–8
  and illness 144 *see also* health, changes in
  personal 176 *see also* marriage
remission, spontaneous 150
resilience 9, 10, 15, 16, 94, 109, 153, 160, 162, 169, 172, 173, 174
risk factors 96
Road Less Travelled, The 16
Rutter, Professor Michael 15, 94, 173

SANDS (Stillbirth and Neonatal Death Society) 158 *see also* Miscarriage Association, The
self-confidence 79, 82, 145, 172, 183 *see also* confidence
self-esteem 9, 24, 39, 82, 85, 107, 133, 149, 172, 174, 184
self-help groups 38, 88, 142, 163
senses 29

separation, negative 173
  happy 174
sexual abuse *see* abuse, childhood sexual
shock 117
sickness *see* health, changes in
Siegel, Bernie 150
skills, listening 163
smoking 30, 36
'steeling' 15
stillbirth *see* loss of baby or child
stress 12, 19
Speck, Peter 146
'superfoods' 31
support 59, 73–4, 147 *see also* self-help groups
surgery 148
survivor sequence 25, 26, 161, 185
sympathy 60

tension, bodily 103 *see also* stress
termination 157
therapy, alternative 38
  cognitive 163
thinking, positive 45, 47
  style of 78
throat, sore 33
thyroid disease 153
tiredness *see* fatigue
turning points 93, 100, 180 *see also* change

ulcers 33

visualisation 151

work 174 *see also* job